12.25.95

Merry Christmas!

Jan

This Book Belongs to

_____

ADDRESS

_____

_____

HOME PHONE

_____

WORK PHONE

_____

FAX

_____

REWARD IF FOUND

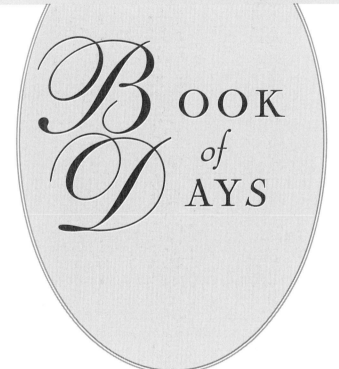

Alexandra Stoddard's

BOOK of DAYS

*E*ach today, well-lived,
makes every yesterday a dream of happiness
and each tomorrow a vision of hope.
Look well, therefore, to this one day,
for it and it alone is life.

—SANSKRIT POEM

Alexandra Stoddard's

BOOK of DAYS

WILLIAM MORROW AND COMPANY, INC.

New York

ISBN:0-688-13686-9

Printed in the United States of America

First Edition

1 2 3 4 5 6 7 8 9 10

DESIGNED BY MARYSARAH QUINN & MARK GAROFALO

Illustrations by Stephen Freeburg

WELCOME

*T*his is your book of life.

*Y*our year begins on the very day you find this book and make it your own. Welcome to this journal. Many joys await you as you put these pages to their best use; think of the ways in which you can turn this into more than a record of doings. Let this journal be a companion to your days and a treasured keepsake to pass down to your grandchildren.

*T*his book has been designed so that you may write down your own Grace Notes—telling clues of your love of life. Use this diary to free your imagination.

I hope your mornings, noontimes, afternoons and evenings are rich with experiences, engagements, appointments, pleasures, contentment and joy. Be open to serendipitous occurrences. Embrace the warmth, care, and kindnesses that others show you. Let every experience expand your awareness of your surroundings and your appreciation of life.

*F*inally, remember that each day is a microcosm of your life. Your positive attitude, your ability to imbue mundane activities with soul, your new directions, inspirations, insights and quests will uplift you and be a positive influence on the people you love and care about. The connections and possibilities are boundless.

*W*elcome to your book of days.

*G*race, joy, and love *every* day of the year.

Alexandra Stoddard

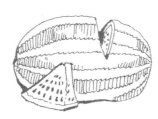

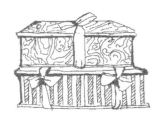

*L*ove begins at home, and it is not how much we do … but how much love we put in that action.

—MOTHER TERESA

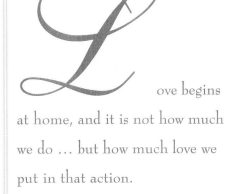

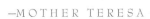

MAKING THE MOST
OF YOUR *BOOK OF DAYS*

*J*ump right in. There is no perfect day or time. Begin wherever you are and move forward. Don't be afraid to write in these beautiful pages, for without your active participation this book is meaningless. The more you use it, the more exciting your days will become. Energy and enthusiasm are infectious. Go for it.

*P*lace the ribbon at the start of each week, and write in the month and date at the top where indicated. If you enjoy using a fountain pen, you'll find this paper sensational. I use my usual fuchsia ink but you may change colors at whim. Experiment. You can use magic markers, colored pencils, ordinary lead pencils or ballpoint pens. It's entirely up to you. The whole point of this is to inspire you to make the most of *every day*.

*M*ark in the time of each appointment, meeting or event. Make notations about the weather, your mood, and what's going on around you. When you get to the end of the week, fill in "The Best Things That Happened This Week" and "Goals for Next Week." Review each day and fill the squares with notes about those special moments that occurred on the appropriate day. Record feelings, or a delicious meal you enjoyed, or a letter that gave you pleasure.

*R*ead the quote and Grace Note of the day and take time to reflect on the message. At the end of the week, reread them and underline the ones that resonate for you.

*A*s you go along, write in your own Grace Notes, the birthdays of people you love, special celebrations, the favorite things of children, lovers and friends, the gifts you plan to give, the gifts stored in your inventory, quotes, affirmations and inspirations, joys, things learned as well as a story that made you laugh. Write about your times of solitude as well as moments shared with others.

*D*oodle, draw, add an extra ribbon or two. Keep a cup of colored pencils close at hand to make sketches. Cross out appointments cancelled or postponed. A full book of days will be your record of a life in process: a courageous, adventurous journey.

*I*n these stressful and troubled times, we are all too busy to *really* live unless we purposely sit back, sip some tea and think about how we want to spend our time, who we want to share it with and then make it happen. Fill in the colorful boxes and live each moment with more zest, more fun and more pure living than ever before.

*H*appy days!   *Alexandra Stoddard*

NEW DIRECTIONS

It is our duty as men and women to proceed as though limits to our ability do not exist. We are collaborators in creation.

TEILHARD DE CHARDIN

Each day we're given a fresh start. Today can be the beginning of a more productive, affirming existence. Let all the pain, regrets, disappointments, and disillusions of yesterday fall from your shoulders. Don't let gray days get you down. Focus on the light. Do not dwell on problems but seek satisfying solutions.

Place a new emphasis on all the goodness in your life, all the blessings you have, your love, your children, your work, your friends, your home. Let your love of life reinforce all you do and let all your energy be used to build a better world, a place where grandchildren may be safe and find joy. Spread hope through your strength and courage and unwavering determination to live a healthy, productive, full life that rises above sorrow and defeat. Light candles, smile, sing out in praise for all you have. Take time to ritualize moments, create ceremonies and celebrations.

Vitality is self-generated. Living in this awareness gives you the energy to go the extra mile, to put your trust in everything you do. Whatever is worth doing deserves your full creative force. Never succumb to mediocrity.

Concentrate on putting some magic into every day. Stretch yourself to find out what is possible and then stretch farther: dare to do the impossible. Tap into the universal energy of love.

Alexandra Stoddard

	SUNDAY	MONDAY	TUESDAY	WEDNESDAY
MORNING	For life was freakish/And life was fervent/And I was always/Life's willing servant. STEPHEN VINCENT BENET			
NOON			Great joys, like griefs, are silent. SHACKERLEY MARMION	
AFTERNOON		We live by admiration, hope and love. WORDSWORTH		One of these days is none of these days. H. G. BOHN
EVENING				
GRACE NOTES	Participate fully in everything you do. The more you care, the more you will accomplish. Go for it!	Make a point of affirming those around you today. Begin with yourself. Offer hope and joy.	There are some epiphanies that radiate and are celebrated internally.	Begin something new today. A poem, a journal, a family ritual. Let today be a special, memorable day.

Month _____ THE WEEK OF _____ TO _____

THURSDAY	FRIDAY	SATURDAY	
	*W*e are not hypocrites in our sleep. WILLIAM HAZLITT		*P*erfect valor is to do without witnesses what one would do before all the world. LA ROCHEFOUCAULD

*P*ersistent work triumphs. VIRGIL

THE BEST THINGS THAT
HAPPENED THIS WEEK:

....
....
....
....
....
....
....

I am never indifferent, and never pretend to be. LONGFELLOW

GOALS
FOR NEXT WEEK:

....
....
....
....
....
....
....

| *Y*ou can never care too much. Enthusiasm is the fire that makes you soar. | *B*e direct. Acknowledge your interests and passions. Be honest with yourself and others. | *E*verything you do with love and focus will have results. Practice patient persistence. | *Y*our thoughts and acts of kindness will shape your character. |

	*S*UNDAY	*M*ONDAY	*T*UESDAY	*W*EDNESDAY
MORNING			*O*ne finds one's own style by finding one's own self. LIN YUTANG	
NOON	*G*reat thoughts come from the heart. LUC DE CLAPIERS			
AFTERNOON				*A*nywhere is paradise. GEORGE HARRISON
EVENING		*A*nd trust me not at all or all in all. TENNYSON		
GRACE NOTES	*W*hat is your heart bursting with today? How are you going to express it?	*S*urround yourself with trustworthy people and don't second-guess them.	*S*tyle is not an outer trapping but an authentic understanding of your essential personality. Style polishes your essence.	*K*eep inside you an image of your ideal place. Whether it be a mountain, a beach or a garden, you *are* there, here.

THURSDAY	FRIDAY	SATURDAY	
		*W*hether you think you can do a thing or not, you're right. HENRY FORD	*A*nyone who keeps the ability to see beauty never grows old. KAFKA
	*T*here is always a better way. THOMAS EDISON		**THE BEST THINGS THAT HAPPENED THIS WEEK:**
			....
I grow old ever learning many things. SOLON			**GOALS FOR NEXT WEEK:**
			....
*M*y husband, Peter, has requested that his tombstone read "Still Learning." What are *you* exploring?	*N*ever settle for the mediocre. Create, invent a better way of living each day.	*F*ollow your convictions. Practice the art of the possible. Stay away from people who tell you what you can't do.	*T*oday, practice seeing everything anew and thus enrich your understanding.

	SUNDAY	MONDAY	TUESDAY	WEDNESDAY
MORNING		*R*ipeness is all. SHAKESPEARE		
NOON			*R*eading is to the mind what exercise is to the body. SIR RICHARD STEELE	
AFTERNOON				*C*haracter is destiny. HERACLITUS
EVENING	*W*here there is no vision, the people perish. PROVERBS 29:18			
GRACE NOTES	*T*he proverb above was once chiseled on the pulpit of New York City's Heavenly Rest Church—inadvertently without the "no." Have vision!	*P*ay attention to ripeness. This applies to tomatoes, avocados, work and love.	*M*ake a list of books you want to read. What are you reading now? Are these books good for your mind? Your soul?	*C*haracter is the essential ingredient that pilots our life. Nothing is more important. Be on watch to evaluate *your* character.

*N*o man can lose what he
never had.   IZAAK WALTON

*W*e can do anything
we want to do if we stick
to it long enough.

HELEN KELLER

I am not arguing with
you—I am telling you.
WHISTLER

THE BEST THINGS THAT
HAPPENED THIS WEEK:

....
....
....
....
....
....
....

*T*he sky is the daily bread of
the eyes.   EMERSON

GOALS
FOR NEXT WEEK:

....
....
....
....
....
....
....

I had an art teacher who
urged us to look up. The sky is
our light and illumination.
The sun is shining somewhere.

*D*on't focus on loss, but on
what you have. Concentrate
on your assets, your good
qualities, your generosity
of spirit.

*P*eople resist hearing the
truth. It sometimes stings. Be
yourself. There are times when
telling the truth *is* necessary.

*A*ll my heroes and
heroines are people who
overcame unspeakable
hardships and triumphed.
They teach us to be tenacious.

	SUNDAY	MONDAY	TUESDAY	WEDNESDAY
MORNING		*K*nowledge is the food of the soul. PLATO		*C*arpe diem. HORACE
NOON	*A*ll intellectual improvement arises from leisure. SAMUEL JOHNSON			
AFTERNOON			*W*hat if this present were the world's last night? JOHN DONNE	
EVENING				
GRACE NOTES	*I*'m wisest on Sundays when I give myself time to think. A day of *businesslessness* is often a great inspirer.	*T*he more we learn, the fuller our soul becomes, and yet there's always room for more.	*L*ive in the consciousness of *now* being the fullness of your existence. This is no ordinary Tuesday, is it?!	*S*eize the day! Seize the moment! Discover the richness of life's possibilities by expecting a lot from yourself.

THURSDAY	FRIDAY	SATURDAY	
			*T*he great enemy of the truth is very often not the lie—deliberate, contrived and dishonest— but the myth—persistent, persuasive and unrealistic. JOHN F. KENNEDY
	*S*omething will turn up. BENJAMIN DISRAELI		THE BEST THINGS THAT HAPPENED THIS WEEK: ....
		*S*ilence is the greatest persecution. PASCAL	
*T*he greatest virtues are those which are most useful to other persons. ARISTOTLE			GOALS FOR NEXT WEEK: ....
*G*o about your day doing your best, going the extra mile. Goodness enriches the life of others.	*K*eep studying. Read. Experiment. Einstein loved his experiments. Be a genius by trying. Seek.	*S*ing out in praise of those you admire, respect and love. And then be silent.	*P*ay attention to reality. Myths can make you miserable. There is plenty to deal with today that is real, immediate and true.

	$\mathcal{S}$UNDAY	$\mathcal{M}$ONDAY	$\mathcal{T}$UESDAY	$\mathcal{W}$EDNESDAY
MORNING	$\mathcal{T}$ime driveth onward fast. TENNYSON			$\mathcal{W}$hat is always speaking silently is the body. NORMAN O. BROWN
NOON		$\mathcal{A}$h, but a man's reach should exceed his grasp, or what's a heaven for? ROBERT BROWNING		
AFTERNOON			$\mathcal{A}$ll the modern inconveniences.　MARK TWAIN	
EVENING				
GRACE NOTES	$\mathcal{W}$e are only given a tiny slice of time. How can you hold time?	$\mathcal{S}$tretching your mind doesn't hurt. Think of what you can begin today that is beyond your grasp. Start it!	$\mathcal{D}$on't have a nervous breakdown over the so-called conveniences that don't work. Be patient!	$\mathcal{P}$ay attention to everything the body tells you. In a sense, you can become your own doctor by taking good care of yourself.

THURSDAY	FRIDAY	SATURDAY	
	*B*ut the sea never explains the flower. EDITH HAMILTON		*W*e are spinning our own fates, good or evil, and never to be undone. Every smallest stroke of virtue or of vice leaves its ever so little scar. … Nothing we ever do is, in strict scientific literalness, wiped out. WILLIAM JAMES

*T*he present is our own.
THOMAS LOVE PEACOCK

THE BEST THINGS THAT
HAPPENED THIS WEEK:

....
....
....
....
....
....
....

I don't want to go out.
I don't want out-ness.
BROOKE STODDARD

GOALS
FOR NEXT WEEK:

....
....
....
....
....
....

*W*hy go out tonight? Stay at home, be private, cozy and surround yourself with books; play music; observe a flower.

*Y*ou will never be able to understand everything. Be yourself and be content.

*A*ll we will ever own or behold with certainty is the moment. Reflect on *now* and *live* on earth while on earth.

*B*e the architect of your fate. Think about everything as interconnecting circles. Life builds in strength, goodness and light. Start drafting.

	ᏚUNDAY	ᎷONDAY	ᎢUESDAY	ᎳEDNESDAY
MORNING			Happiness is no laughing matter. ARCHBISHOP RICHARD WHATELEY	
NOON				Come up and see me sometime. MAE WEST
AFTERNOON		He begins to die that quits his desires. GEORGE HERBERT		
EVENING	The feast of reason and the flow of the soul. ALEXANDER POPE			
GRACE NOTES	Whenever we are reasonable, we are nurturing our soul. Trust common sense. Be in the flow of love.	Live with expanding, grand, great desires. Plant a tree the day you die. Desire to live forever. You just may.	Happy people are our teachers, for they have had to overcome all their obstacles. They are spreaders of hope for all of us.	Call a friend today; make a date for a visit. Come see me sometime.

Thursday

Friday

To every thing there is a
season, and a time to every
purpose under the heaven.
ECCLESIASTES

Saturday

*N*othing is little to
him that feels it with
great sensibility.
SAMUEL JOHNSON

THE BEST THINGS THAT
HAPPENED THIS WEEK:

....
....
....
....
....
....
....

*O*nly the educated are free.
EPICTETUS

*W*hat I aspired to be, And
was not, comforts me.
ROBERT BROWNING

GOALS
FOR NEXT WEEK:

....
....
....
....
....
....
....

*N*o one, nothing can
keep us from our journey.
Searching, questing will
assure a vital life: Education is
the result.

*N*ow is the time to bring
together your fresh interests
with your innate talents and
strengths so they may have
time to be fulfilled.

*E*xpect greatness and settle
for being as good as you can
be, as caring as an angel.

*F*eeling everything with a
sense of awe can elevate the
quiet, private experience into a
sacred moment.

Month _____ THE WEEK OF _____ TO _____

	SUNDAY	MONDAY	TUESDAY	WEDNESDAY
MORNING			There is a good within each human breast. OVID	
NOON	Remember when life's path is steep to keep your mind even. HORACE			
AFTERNOON				Every religion is good that teaches man to be good. THOMAS PAINE
EVENING		May you live all the days of your life. JONATHAN SWIFT		
GRACE NOTES	When you are experiencing your greatest hardship, choose to concentrate on your own unwavering purpose.	Make today one of those magic days in whch you do an abundance of really wonderful things. What will you do?	Find it. When someone is driving you crazy, light a candle and write down their virtues.	Embrace each truly good human soul. Don't judge how the wisdom came into consciousness. Goodness is universal.

THURSDAY	FRIDAY	SATURDAY	
			*M*arriage is not a goal in itself but is simply another opportunity to grow and mature. GOETHE
*C*ulture has one great passion —the passion for sweetness and light. MATTHEW ARNOLD			THE BEST THINGS THAT HAPPENED THIS WEEK: ....
		*D*o the thing and you will be given the power. EMERSON	
	*T*is to create, and in creating live. LORD BYRON		GOALS FOR NEXT WEEK: ....
*T*here's darkness and despair in the world. Your radiance will light the way.	*W*hen you create something unique, you give birth to *your* humanity. Create something beautiful today. What?	*W*hen you know what has to be expressed, do it. Strength is always there when you're willing to dare.	*I*n my husband, Peter, I have found my other half. Our lives double in growth and possibility. Partnership is the key.

	⟨Sunday⟩	⟨Monday⟩	⟨Tuesday⟩	⟨Wednesday⟩
MORNING				
NOON		$\mathcal{R}$ather than love, than money, than fame, give me truth. THOREAU		
AFTERNOON	$\mathcal{L}$ife has got to be lived— that's all there is to it. ELEANOR ROOSEVELT			$\mathcal{A}$sk not for whom the bell tolls; it tolls for thee. JOHN DONNE
EVENING			$\mathcal{M}$eet me by moonlight alone. JOSEPH AUGUSTINE WADE	
GRACE NOTES	$\mathcal{L}$ife must be fully experienced. If it appears easy today, rest assured it will be difficult tomorrow. Live *all of it* for total satisfaction.	$\mathcal{T}$ruth is a quest that helps one understand life's potential. Grace, love and light are true. Believe that truth.	$\mathcal{W}$e're lucky if we ever meet our true love. Who have you met or will you meet by moonlight alone?	$\mathcal{W}$hatever good you do in your corner of the world will ring bells across the universe. Let a ringing bell inspire you to act.

Month _____ THE WEEK OF _____ TO _____

THURSDAY	FRIDAY	SATURDAY	
*C*ourage is resistance to fear. MARK TWAIN			*I*f a man empties his purse into his head, no one can take it away from him. An investment in knowledge always pays the best interest. BENJAMIN FRANKLIN
		*T*he unexamined life is not worth living. SOCRATES	THE BEST THINGS THAT HAPPENED THIS WEEK: ....
	*T*ruth must be conceived as a truth. ALBERT EINSTEIN		
			GOALS FOR NEXT WEEK: ....
*L*iving is a courageous act. Dare to face challenges head on and then feel grace.	*W*illiam James believed truth is what works. Believe in what you see, the ordinary, the familiar, as long as they ring true.	*A*ll insight is acquired slowly. We must consciously examine our lives every day and monitor our paths.	*L*earning is a sure bet. It's exciting and it puts life's setbacks into perspective. What are you studying now?

	*S*UNDAY	*M*ONDAY	*T*UESDAY	*W*EDNESDAY
MORNING	*S*ilent gratitude isn't much use to anyone. GLADYS BERTHE STERN			
NOON		*E*ven a small start is worth a try. SENATOR JOHN DANFORTH		
AFTERNOON				*E*very day is a New Year. ROSE MARIE MORSE
EVENING			*L*ife shrinks or expands in proportion to one's courage. ANAÏS NIN	
GRACE NOTES	*T*he most appropriate time to tell someone what you think of them is at the time you extend your thanks. Praise must be expressed generously and immediately.	*T*he greatest failure of all is the idea never put to use. Start today. Spare yourself the sadness of what might have been.	*B*eing brave is more important than being brilliant. Brave people usually get all they need from life. Courage brings joy.	*E*mbrace every dawn as an opportunity for illumination, inspiration, insight and personal growth.

THURSDAY	FRIDAY	SATURDAY	
*F*atigue makes cowards of us all. VINCE LOMBARDI			*I* never think of the future. It comes soon enough. ALBERT EINSTEIN
			THE BEST THINGS THAT HAPPENED THIS WEEK: ....
		M an can never escape from himself. GOETHE	
	F ind the good—and praise it. ALEX HALEY		GOALS FOR NEXT WEEK: ....
W hen our energy circuits are unplugged, we're unbrave. We feel like crawling under our sheets. Rest up so you can be courageous again.	*L* ook around you. Express gratitude to people, places and things when you find good. This is wisdom.	*Y* our attitude, your character, your every quality goes with you wherever you journey through life. Embrace, don't escape yourself.	*Y* ou and I will never wake up tomorrow. Today is what we have. The future is made of present moments. Think of *now*.

	SUNDAY	MONDAY	TUESDAY	WEDNESDAY
MORNING	*O*ne may measure small things by great. VIRGIL			
NOON			*H*abit is a sort of second nature. CICERO	
AFTERNOON				
EVENING		*T*he mode by which the inevitable comes to pass is effort. OLIVER WENDELL HOLMES		*I* will be *I!* THOREAU
GRACE NOTES	*T*here is no such thing as a small thing. Everything is vitally important—the sun, the shadow, the wind and your smile.	*W*henever we move our feet we are rewarded. That's all there is to it: perseverance.	*L*ook to acquire life-enhancing habits: We are, after all, what we do. Be noble in your habits. They will enrich you.	*T*he faster we focus on who we are, the greater the chance of living a life of significance.

Month _____ THE WEEK OF _____ TO _____

THURSDAY	FRIDAY	SATURDAY	
		There is nothing so advantageous to a man as a forgiving disposition. TERENCE	One great, strong, unselfish soul in every community could actually redeem the world. ELBERT HUBBARD

If you would judge, understand.   SENECA

THE BEST THINGS THAT HAPPENED THIS WEEK:

....
....
....
....
....
....

Whatever your advice, make it brief.   HORACE

GOALS
FOR NEXT WEEK:

❧..
....
....
....
❧..
....
....

No one wants to hear a long, drawn-out story of what should be done. Make your point and let go.

Think of yourself as a mirror. Everything you think, feel and judge could be you.

Forgive and forget. Every day should potentially be a fresh start.

Reflect on all the giving souls you know who make a difference. What is it about their spirit that makes them shine?

	Sunday	Monday	Tuesday	Wednesday
MORNING		*D*on't find fault, find a remedy. HENRY FORD		
NOON	*U*nto ourselves our own life is necessary; unto others, our character. ST. AUGUSTINE			
AFTERNOON				*W*e cannot go back. WITOLD RYBCZYNSKI
EVENING			*E*very noble work is, at first, impossible. THOMAS CARLYLE	
GRACE NOTES	*W*hether we like it or not, our actions reveal our character. Good deeds speak of integrity. Be decent and life will be beautiful.	*E*veryone is quick to point out problems. What's noble is to find solutions. This is an ongoing challenge. What are your solutions for today?	*E*verything appears too difficult until we commit ourselves. Don't dream scared. Dream of the impossible and work miracles into your life.	*S*ift through the sands of your past to find the gold. Look at it, don't carry it; travel light.

Month _____ THE WEEK OF _____ TO _____

THURSDAY	FRIDAY	SATURDAY	

*I*t is no use saying "We are doing our best." You have got to succeed in doing what is necessary.

WINSTON CHURCHILL

*A*sk, and it shall be given you; seek, and ye shall find; knock, and it shall be opened unto you.   MATTHEW 7:7

THE BEST THINGS THAT HAPPENED THIS WEEK:

....
....
....
....
....
....
....

*H*appiness and beauty are by-products.

GEORGE BERNARD SHAW

*W*hile we teach, we learn.

SENECA

GOALS FOR NEXT WEEK:

....
....
....
....
....
....

*A*n artist friend wrote books to learn about a subject. We gain inspiration from those we instruct.

*B*e willing to ask for help. Whether you pray or seek, let life show you its abundance. Ask.

*W*henever we follow in the path of our beliefs, we will discover more richness than we could ever seek or ask for.

*F*ind new ways to do the best work for the common good. Success is the result of doing whatever has to be done.

Month _____ THE WEEK OF _____ TO _____

	SUNDAY	***M***ONDAY	***T***UESDAY	***W***EDNESDAY
MORNING			***A***lways and in everything let there be reverence. CONFUCIUS	
NOON				
AFTERNOON		***T***he measure of a civilization is the degree of its obedience to the unenforceable. LORD MOULTON		***W***hat does rain taste like? SARAH MIDORI ZIMMERMAN
EVENING	***I***deals become starchy habits. CARL JUNG			
GRACE NOTES	***W***hat are your goals for the week? Think noble thoughts and one good, noble thing will lead to another.	***W***e do certain things automatically because we believe they are right. What is a matter of personal honor to you?	***O***ur attitude constitutes all the difference between the perfunctory and the sacred. Revere everything today. Bliss follows.	***W***hen was the last time you took a walk in the rain?

THURSDAY

*A*ll the arts are essentially one.   JOHN LA FARGE

*E*verything can inspire if it is essentially beautiful. Live the art spirit; it is one.

FRIDAY

*A*ll things are changed, and we change with them.
LOTHAIR I

*E*verything is constantly changing. We can improve our lives every day. Respect the past; live in the present.

SATURDAY

*K*nowledge of the possible is the beginning of happiness.
GEORGE SANTAYANA

*O*pportunities for great achievement present themselves every day. Think positively of all you want to accomplish. Just do it and be happy.

*P*hilosophy has the task and the opportunity of helping banish the concept that human destiny here and now is of slight importance in comparison with some supernatural destiny.
JOHN DEWEY

THE BEST THINGS THAT HAPPENED THIS WEEK:

....
....
....
....
....
....
....

GOALS
FOR NEXT WEEK:

❧..
....
....
....
❧..
....
....

*M*ake a point of finding meaning and purpose in your life. What are your gifts? How will you use them?

	$\mathcal{S}$UNDAY	$\mathcal{M}$ONDAY	$\mathcal{T}$UESDAY	$\mathcal{W}$EDNESDAY
MORNING	$\mathcal{H}$e who weighs his responsibilities can bear them. MARTIAL			
NOON		$\mathcal{W}$e all like people who do things. WILLA CATHER		
AFTERNOON				$\mathcal{W}$e think in generalities, but we live in detail. ALFRED NORTH WHITEHEAD
EVENING			$\mathcal{O}$riginality is simply a new pair of eyes. THOMAS WENTWORTH HIGGINSON	
GRACE NOTES	$\mathcal{R}$esponsibility means being accountable, dependable and independent. Embrace your responsibilities.	$\mathcal{E}$veryone who achieves some recognition has worked hard. Committed, passionate people inspire us with their energy.	$\mathcal{T}$oday, look and *really* see every object in your bedroom, bath and kitchen. When we see life uniquely, we will express originality at home.	$\mathcal{D}$etails add up to wholeness. Pay careful attention to every detail. Details are the building blocks of beauty.

Thursday	*Friday*	*Saturday*	
		Secure, whate'er he gives, he gives the best. SAMUEL JOHNSON	*A man without decision can never be said to belong to himself.* JOHN FOSTER
Good is not good, where better is expected. THOMAS FULLER			**THE BEST THINGS THAT HAPPENED THIS WEEK:**
	Fortune favors the brave. TERENCE		
			GOALS FOR NEXT WEEK:
Do the best you can, no matter what the task. Satisfaction comes from going the extra mile. Expect excellence.	*Whenever we are courageous, we are given the strength to overcome obstacles. Bravery builds and prepares you to take more risks.*	*Give your all. Don't hold back.*	*Live choicefully. Know what is right for you and what isn't. You will never feel serenity unless you are able to make choices without guilt.*

INSPIRATIONS

Take your own life, every one of you.

EDITH WHARTON

What are some of the most inspiring things that have happened to you these past three months? Have you embarked on a new, exciting voyage? Remember, there is no one path. Each one of us is capable of exploring ways to live with more grace, joy and love. What are you most passionate about right now? What thrills you?

Our life is made up of moments. Cumulatively, what we do to fill our time, how we approach each day, what we do to carve out some solitude for reflection, private pleasures and delights makes up a life. Think of this book of days as your story, broken up into chapters and parts. You are living the story and recording it. We are all authors, creators of our own reality.

What are you reading that exhilarates you? Who are some of your favorite authors? What are you most excited about studying now? I'm reading the Fifth Edition of the *Columbia Encyclopedia*. I'm stunned at my ignorance and thrilled to expand my horizons.

What are the things you were once crazy about? Take up something you have put aside in the rush of life; seek continuity. Engage in projects that are yours alone. Stamp collecting, painting, writing poetry, or bird watching will bring a spark of joy when rediscovered.

Who have you heard lecture or perform that inspired you to live more deeply? I cried with joy watching Sam Waterston act in *Abe Lincoln in Illinois*. When was the last time you were so swept away that you had an almost out-of-body experience, forgetting time and place?

What do you do that puts you in the flow of life, that fills you with joy and a sense of love, peace and contentment?

	SUNDAY	MONDAY	TUESDAY	WEDNESDAY
MORNING			*H*ealth is the thing that makes you feel that now is the best time of the year. FRANKLIN P. ADAMS	
NOON	*I* believe in an ultimate decency of things. ROBERT LOUIS STEVENSON			
AFTERNOON		*T*he poet should prefer probable impossibilities to improbable possibilities. ARISTOTLE		
EVENING				*P*hilosophy is nothing but discretion. JOHN SELDEN
GRACE NOTES	*D*on't lose faith. Stay on your path and do everything with a sense of decency and fairness. Live like a poet.	*T*he poet is attracted to seeing the possibilities in the impossibilities.	*A* quick mental health tip: The more you absorb yourself in each day, each season, the more vibrant you will be.	*W*e all have to develop a point of view about life, set limits and commit ourselves to pursue the good. Be a truth seeker.

THURSDAY

FRIDAY

SATURDAY

It is life near the bone where it is sweetest.   THOREAU

Seize this very minute. What you can do or dream, you can begin it. Boldness has genius, power and magic in it.

GOETHE

THE BEST THINGS THAT HAPPENED THIS WEEK:

....
....
....
....
....
....
....

Audacity, more audacity, and always audacity.   DANTON

For if the talent or individuality is there, it should be expressed.

SHIRLEY MACLAINE

GOALS
FOR NEXT WEEK:

⤙..
....
....
....
⤙..
....
....

What is burning inside you that you want to bring to life? Don't wait for an ideal time. Begin today to express something unique.

Be bold. Express your style. Wear brightly colored stockings. Or sprightly ties.

The more I simplify, the more pleasure I feel. Learn the art of NO. Practice it regularly. Simplicity is blessed.

I love starting something new, not having any idea where it will lead me. Feel the power and magic of boldness.

Month _____ THE WEEK OF _____ TO _____

	SUNDAY	MONDAY	TUESDAY	WEDNESDAY
MORNING	*W*hat I tell you three times is true. LEWIS CARROLL			*S*pend all you have for loveliness. SARA TEASDALE
NOON			*N*ot too much zeal. TALLEYRAND	
AFTERNOON				
EVENING		*T*he secret to writing is writing. WRITERS' BOOT CAMP		
GRACE NOTES	*B*e consistent in purpose and instructions. Repeat for emphasis and emotional impact. Say "I love you" and "Thank you" often.	*W*riters write. It's more than discipline or habit. It is a need, like breathing. The more you write, the more content you are.	*R*emain open to new ideas. Embrace with an open mind.	*B*eauty is priceless. Enduring beauty is a form of immortality. No effort or sacrifice is wasted when you create loveliness.

THURSDAY	FRIDAY	SATURDAY	

A happy life must be to a great extent a quiet life, for it is only in an atmosphere of quiet that true joy can live.

BERTRAND RUSSELL

THE BEST THINGS THAT HAPPENED THIS WEEK:

....

....

....

....

....

....

....

*F*or every disciplined effort there is a multiple reward.

JIM ROHN

*T*he fusion of energy between the audience and the performer is God.

AGNES DE MILLE

GOALS
FOR NEXT WEEK:

....

....

....

....

....

....

*C*haracter is higher than intellect.

EMERSON

*W*hen you stretch your envelope, work *really* hard, rewards usually follow. The secret is to see something through to the end. Press on.

*T*here are many intelligent people who, unhappily, are corrupt. Value people you can trust, who have good character above all else.

*W*hat was the last stunning performance you saw? Did you feel the energy?

*H*appiness requires balance among tension, quiet and grace.

	$\mathcal{S}$UNDAY	$\mathcal{M}$ONDAY	$\mathcal{T}$UESDAY	$\mathcal{W}$EDNESDAY
MORNING	*No act of kindness, no matter how small, is ever wasted.* AESOP			
NOON		*Rhythm provides the cadence of life.* PETER MEGARGEE BROWN		
AFTERNOON			*Never tell your resolutions beforehand.* JOHN SELDEN	
EVENING				*He gives twice who gives soon.* PUBLILIUS SYRUS
GRACE NOTES	*The smallest thing you do to show you care holds great power. Act on every impulse to love.*	*When we stay in the natural flow of time we feel balanced and in harmony. Feel your rhythm. Never rush.*	*Talk is easier than action. Better move in the direction of your goals privately. Telling doesn't necessarily help.*	*A short thank-you note is better than a long, delayed letter full of excuses. Be an earth angel and give soon.*

THURSDAY

FRIDAY

SATURDAY

The room is full of you!
EDNA ST. VINCENT MILLAY

The happiest people
in this world are those
who have the most
interesting thoughts.
WILLIAM LYON PHELPS

We two form a multitude.
OVID

THE BEST THINGS THAT
HAPPENED THIS WEEK:

....
....
....
....
....
....
....

Appreciation is
yeast, lifting ordinary to
extraordinary.
MARY-ANN PETRO

GOALS
FOR NEXT WEEK:

....
....
....
....
....
....
....

Look around you at all the remarkable wonders in your midst: the sunrise, the sunset, a child, a flower. Appreciate what you have.

When two people find their other halves, their love can inspire everyone around them. Grow in strength and light together.

Spaces speak of their occupants. Let your rooms radiate your essence, your grace and your love.

When we are able to amuse ourselves with fresh insights and ideas, we are never bored. Happiness is a result of exploring your mind.

Month ———————————— THE WEEK OF ———————————— TO ————————————

	*S*UNDAY	*M*ONDAY	*T*UESDAY	*W*EDNESDAY
MORNING				
NOON			*L* earn that the present hour alone is man's. SAMUEL JOHNSON	
AFTERNOON	*A* ll good things which exist are the fruits of originality. JOHN STUART MILL			*E* very new adjustment is a crisis in self-esteem. ERIC HOFFER
EVENING		*S* orrow and silence are strong, and patient endurance is godlike. LONGFELLOW		
GRACE NOTES	*E* very fresh thought forges new trails. Dare to explore new territory and make it your own.	*W* e learn to be courageous from those who suffer yet never complain.	*D* on't let anyone rob you of your present hour. Put this time to wise use that will bring lasting results and satisfactions.	*T* hink of a new situation as a challenge. How can you help someone else to get through a transition smoothly?

$\mathscr{T}$HURSDAY

$\mathscr{I}$ bend but do not break.
JEAN DE LA FONTAINE

$\mathscr{W}$e must remain flexible and agile in all matters. Bend. You won't crack; you will remain whole.

$\mathscr{F}$RIDAY

$\mathscr{T}$he half is greater than the whole. HESIOD

$\mathscr{C}$ut back. Simplify. Be selective in all you take in and take on. No one gets it all. Half can literally make you whole.

$\mathscr{S}$ATURDAY

$\mathscr{K}$nowledge is a fine thing. MOLIÈRE

$\mathscr{L}$earning keeps us curious, young and vital. What are you studying up on now? What do you find fascinating?

$\mathscr{C}$an anyone understand how it is to have lived in the White House, and then, suddenly, to be living alone as the President's widow?

JACQUELINE KENNEDY

THE BEST THINGS THAT HAPPENED THIS WEEK:

....
....
....
....
....
....
....

GOALS FOR NEXT WEEK:

....
....
....
....
....
....
....

$\mathscr{F}$ew of us can understand another's life. Tragedy and sudden loss can happen to any of us. Sympathize. Empathize.

	Sunday	*Monday*	*Tuesday*	*Wednesday*
MORNING	*Envy is a kind of praise.* JOHN JAY			
NOON				*Mount, mount, my soul!* SHAKESPEARE
AFTERNOON		*All greatness is unconscious.* THOMAS CARLYLE		
EVENING			*All are needed by each one; Nothing is fair or good alone.* EMERSON	
GRACE NOTES	*What have you done that is worthy of envy?*	*The wisest, most talented people are often the most humble. Use naturally all God gave you.*	*We need each other. Think of all the people who add richness to your life. Who has helped you the most? We're all intertwined.*	*Think of your life's journey as a lightness of being. We can shed the weights that bog us down, the stress and strains of the ego.*

THURSDAY

I live and love in God's
peculiar light.   MICHELANGELO

FRIDAY

A snow year, a rich year.
GEORGE HERBERT

SATURDAY

L ife here and now
would be all right if only
you looked at it a little
differently.   GEORGE ORWELL

THE BEST THINGS THAT
HAPPENED THIS WEEK:

....
....
....
....
....
....
....

T rust your heart.
JUDY COLLINS

GOALS
FOR NEXT WEEK:

....
....
....
....
....
....
....

B e a light-seeker and a
light-bearer. Envision a candle
burning brightly in the center
of your being. Spread the
radiance.

C laude Monet loved to
paint snow scenes as well as
abundant gardens. Bless the
four seasons.

Y our feelings never lie.
Pay attention to the tugs.
Think of angels and act as one.
Heartfelt actions are angelic.

B y changing our attitude
and perspective we can create
epiphanies in the least likely
places. Dwell on life's
possibilities.

Month _____ THE WEEK OF _____ TO _____

	SUNDAY	MONDAY	TUESDAY	WEDNESDAY
MORNING		Saying is one thing, and doing is another. MONTAIGNE		
NOON			I saw and loved. EDWARD GIBBON	
AFTERNOON				Excellent things are rare. PLATO
EVENING	In goodness there are all kinds of wisdom. EURIPIDES			
GRACE NOTES	It is always wise to be good. Express your goodness in your own way, on your own terms. When you're good, you're always right.	When I was younger I promised. Now, I do my best. Be a doer, silently.	What have you seen recently that left you in awe? True love is sacred, beautiful and true. Look, realize and love.	Everyone is not equal in their ability to be excellent. We can all be good, and that's all that matters.

$\mathcal{T}$HURSDAY

$\mathcal{T}$o think is to live. CICERO

$\mathcal{F}$RIDAY

$\mathcal{S}$ATURDAY

$\mathcal{T}$here is always hope for an individual who stops to do some serious thinking about life.

KATHERINE LOGAN

THE BEST THINGS THAT HAPPENED THIS WEEK:

....
....
....
....
....
....
....

$\mathcal{W}$here there is charity and wisdom, there is neither fear nor ignorance.

ST. FRANCIS OF ASSISI

GOALS
FOR NEXT WEEK:

....
....
....
....
....
....
....

$\mathcal{W}$hatever is worth doing at all, is worth doing well.

LORD CHESTERFIELD

$\mathcal{Y}$ou have power over your own thoughts. The quality of what you think determines the quality of your life. Think lofty thoughts.

$\mathcal{D}$oing anything worthwhile requires time and patience. When we enjoy what we're doing, we shed stress and satisfaction abounds.

$\mathcal{F}$ear comes from lack of faith in life's basic goodness. Make an effort to give back to the world and fear will go away.

$\mathcal{L}$ife requires serious reflection. The more you think, the deeper your journey.

Month _____ THE WEEK OF _____ TO _____

	$\mathscr{S}$UNDAY	$\mathscr{M}$ONDAY	$\mathscr{T}$UESDAY	$\mathscr{W}$EDNESDAY
MORNING		$\mathscr{L}$ife makes great demands on people's characters. IVY COMPTON-BURNETT		
NOON			$\mathscr{T}$ake up, read! Take up, read! ST. AUGUSTINE	
AFTERNOON	$\mathscr{T}$he secret of success is constancy of purpose. BENJAMIN DISRAELI			$\mathscr{T}$he only reward of virtue is virtue. EMERSON
EVENING				
GRACE NOTES	$\mathscr{E}$veryone who has fire in their bellies will find their purpose. Once you determine it, stick with your vision.	$\mathscr{W}$e are all tempted at times to do something we would not be proud of. Remember, character is also built by saying NO.	$\mathscr{R}$eading books written by wise men is the best tutoring there is. Sunshine, books and flowers bring joy.	$\mathscr{T}$he good we do feels good. The award, the prize, is to be useful to others, using our unique talents. Reward yourself.

THURSDAY

FRIDAY

SATURDAY

*I*t matters not how a man dies, but how he lives.

SAMUEL JOHNSON

I find the great thing in this world is not so much where we stand, as in what direction we are moving.

OLIVER WENDELL HOLMES

*I*f you wish to draw tears from me, you must first feel pain yourself.　　HORACE

THE BEST THINGS THAT HAPPENED THIS WEEK:

....
....
....
....
....
....
....

A man he seems of cheerful yesterdays.

WORDSWORTH

GOALS FOR NEXT WEEK:

....
....
....
....
....
....
....

*W*e wear our dispositions on our faces. Cheerfulness is a habit; cultivate it. People will be attracted to you.

*W*e are far more capable of hurting ourselves than others. When we are angry, we are the anger's first victim.

*P*eople spend precious time thinking about life after death. I'm far more interested in this life. Live while you're alive.

*E*verything builds. By our daily actions we welcome a fulfilling future. We are not defined by our present situation but by our vision.

	*S*UNDAY	*M*ONDAY	*T*UESDAY	*W*EDNESDAY
MORNING			*E*verything flows. HERACLITUS	
NOON	*L*ife is not living, but living in health. MARTIAL			
AFTERNOON		*A*ll who joy would win/ Must share it,—Happiness was born a twin. BYRON		
EVENING				*W*hen one is pretending the entire body revolts. ANAÏS NIN
GRACE NOTES	*W*e can work on our wellness by allowing serenity into our lives. Meditate and exercise.	*R*each out to give a love pat. Take a walk together. Share a sunset. Hold hands. Star gaze.	*E*verything is moving. Point it in the direction of your dreams. Then, go with the flow. But first, dream big dreams.	*W*henever we are untrue to ourselves and our nature, there is stress to our immune system. The body always knows.

THURSDAY

FRIDAY

SATURDAY

*B*elieve and succeed.
NORMAN VINCENT PEALE

*H*e who controls others may be powerful, but he who has mastered himself is mightier still.

LAO-TZU

*F*or this relief, much thanks.
SHAKESPEARE

THE BEST THINGS THAT HAPPENED THIS WEEK:

....
....
....
....
....
....
....

*Y*ou must do the things you think you cannot do.
ELEANOR ROOSEVELT

GOALS FOR NEXT WEEK:

....
....
....
....
....
....
....

*W*henever something awful happens, we think the pain will last forever. Remember to be thankful when you're given the grace of relief.

*D*on't listen to anyone who says you can't do something. All anything takes is concentration, dedication and luck.

*W*hen you believe in yourself and do your best, success follows. Have faith in what your heart dictates.

*P*eople who live in harmony with themselves have no need to control others. We should all work on ourselves.

	*S*UNDAY	*M*ONDAY	*T*UESDAY	*W*EDNESDAY
MORNING		*E*very man is eloquent once in his life. EMERSON		*I* accept the universe! MARGARET FULLER
NOON			*A*ll good things are cheap; all bad are very dear. THOREAU	
AFTERNOON				
EVENING	*A* single sunbeam is enough to drive away many shadows. ST. FRANCIS OF ASSISI			
GRACE NOTES	*B*e a ray of light in a dark corner of the universe. A smile, an encouraging word, an invitation or a letter spread joy.	*T*here are times when we are unusually articulate. Write down your thoughts. What has brought on this clarity?	*H*ave you noticed that the things that give you pleasure cost you nothing?	*A*cceptance is essential in a well-adapted person. By embracing the universe we expand our potential. Think globally and be accepting.

Thursday	*Friday*	*Saturday*	

*T*o have lived without glory, without leaving a trace of one's existence, is not to have lived at all.

NAPOLEON

*W*hen you're finished changing, you're finished.
BENJAMIN FRANKLIN

THE BEST THINGS THAT HAPPENED THIS WEEK:

....
....
....
....
....
....
....

*T*he soul is for the most part outside the body.   JUNG

*T*oo kind—too kind.
FLORENCE NIGHTINGALE

**GOALS
FOR NEXT WEEK:**

❧..
....
....
....
❧..
....
....

*W*e don't have to know how or where the soul operates. What matters is that we acknowledge the need to nourish our soul.

*R*ecognition for heoric performance often comes late, if at all. Be grateful for having been given the opportunity. The reward is in the doing.

*C*hange is growth. Check yourself regularly to be sure you haven't frozen yourself in a time warp.

*G*lory and triumph require vision, discipline and luck. How do you envision the trace you'll leave of your existence?

Month _____ THE WEEK OF _____ TO _____

	SUNDAY	MONDAY	TUESDAY	WEDNESDAY
MORNING	*The superfluous, a very necessary thing.* VOLTAIRE			
NOON				*Time and chance happeneth to them all.* ECCLESIASTES 9:11
AFTERNOON		*The world is large, but in us it is deep as the sea.* RAINER MARIA RILKE		
EVENING			*Every man is like the company he keeps.* LORD CHESTERFIELD	
GRACE NOTES	*A little luxury may be a necessary extra. Porcelain, flowers, perfume, wine, embroidery, crystal and silver are enhancements of living.*	*We contain the world inside us. As individuals we see and experience its depth in a personal way. How large and how deep is your world?*	*The people around us influence us. The better the company, the more you learn and grow. Surround yourself with superior people.*	*All of us experience our own journey. We think we are alone but everyone travels the same route.*

THURSDAY

I expect I shall be a student to the end of my days.
CHEKHOV

I usually carry a tote bag full of books, notebooks and clippings. Wherever I go, I'm stimulated and excited about what's around the corner.

FRIDAY

*O*ur life is frittered away by detail. Simplify, simplify.
THOREAU

*C*onstant activity? When will we ever find real peace? Be selective in your activities. Simplify.

SATURDAY

*H*ear the other side.
LORD CHESTERFIELD

*T*here are more than two sides to everything. Open up to what I have to tell you. I want to hear your view. Tell me.

---

*C*ome to the edge, he said. They said, We are afraid. Come to the edge, he said. They came. He pushed them…and they flew.
APOLLINAIRE

THE BEST THINGS THAT
HAPPENED THIS WEEK:

....
....
....
....
....
....
....

GOALS
FOR NEXT WEEK:

....
....
....
....
....
....
....

*W*hy are we so afraid of the unknown? When we dare, we often discover a whole new world. Challenge yourself to do something noble.

	*S*UNDAY	*M*ONDAY	*T*UESDAY	*W*EDNESDAY
MORNING	*T*o know and not to do is not yet to know. ZEN SAYING			
NOON			*L*ove him, or leave him alone! WORDSWORTH	
AFTERNOON				*A* wise man never loses anything if he has himself. MONTAIGNE
EVENING		*T*he doors of wisdom are never shut. BENJAMIN YOUNG		
GRACE NOTES	*O*nly when we act do we show that we know. Aristotle taught active virtue. Act on truth.	*B*e a sponge. Open new doors wherever you go. Wisdom comes in the cracks, when you are exploring.	*I*f you can't be loving, kind, sweet and generous, be silent. No one wants or needs to hear anything nasty. Nag not or go.	*W*e will never be able to please everyone. Life is not a popularity contest. Be true to what you hold dear.

THURSDAY	FRIDAY	SATURDAY	

*C*ertain gestures made in childhood seem to have eternal repercussions.
ANAÏS NIN

*T*he hole and the patch should be commensurate.
THOMAS JEFFERSON

THE BEST THINGS THAT HAPPENED THIS WEEK:

....
....
....
....
....
....
....

A moment's insight is sometime's worth a life's experience.
OLIVER WENDELL HOLMES

A letter is a deliberate and written conversation.
BALTASAR GRACIÁN

GOALS
FOR NEXT WEEK:

....
....
....
....
....
....
....

*D*on't make a bigger deal out of something than it is. We should try not to exaggerate; deal with the reality.

*S*uddenly we have a flash of illumination that clarifies everything. Be alert to what Virginia Woolf called "a moment of being."

I'm able to say things in a letter I might never be able to say in conversation. Write a letter and communicate your feelings.

*T*hings we experienced when we were young affect our entire lives. Sift through those memories and concentrate on the positive ones.

	*S*UNDAY	*M*ONDAY	*T*UESDAY	*W*EDNESDAY
MORNING		*O*ne is not born a genius, one becomes a genius. SIMONE DE BEAUVOIR		
NOON	*N*othing is more revealing than movement. MARTHA GRAHAM			
AFTERNOON				*P*erfection belongs to an imaginary world. THOMAS MOORE
EVENING			*B*odies never lie. AGNES DE MILLE	
GRACE NOTES	*W*hen is the last time you danced? Dancing is so freeing. Think of yourself as a dancer and revel in graceful movement.	*O*ur brain is akin to a muscle and needs exercise. Use it or lose it.	*T*aking good care of ourselves requires being aware of the changes that occur gradually. Minor adjustments can prevent illness.	*I*'ve changed my attitude about perfection. Its attainability is a myth that keeps us from our goals. No person or thing is perfect.

*T*HURSDAY	*F*RIDAY	*S*ATURDAY	

*S*ome natural sorrow, loss, or pain/That has been, and may be again.   WORDSWORTH

*Y*es, if you want to say that I was a drum major, say that I was a drum major for justice; say that I was a drum major for peace; I was a drum major for righteousness.

MARTIN LUTHER KING, JR.

*F*aith is the substance of things hoped for, the evidence of things not seen.

HEBREWS 11:1

THE BEST THINGS THAT
HAPPENED THIS WEEK:

....
....
....
....
....
....
....

*I*t is possible to go wrong in many ways, but right in only one.   ARISTOTLE

GOALS
FOR NEXT WEEK:

❧...
....
....
....
❧...
....
....

*T*he more I explore the mystery, the deeper I grow in faith. We will never fully understand. Faith is our ladder to immortality.

*T*here are endless opportunities to mess up. Trust your instincts, and you'll always *know* right from wrong.

*W*hy is it that people who have been through the most difficulty are healers? Life experiences make us courageous or cowards.

*W*hat cause compels you to beat your drum? Is it hunger or education? Is it ecology or wellness? Focus on your passionate concerns next week.

	SUNDAY	MONDAY	TUESDAY	WEDNESDAY
MORNING			$\mathcal{M}$an is what he believes. CHEKHOV	
NOON	$\mathcal{I}$ am a man, I count nothing human indifferent to me. LORD CHESTERFIELD			
AFTERNOON		$\mathcal{W}$e must preserve our right to think and differ. ELEANOR ROOSEVELT		
EVENING				$\mathcal{N}$o cross, no crown. WILLIAM PENN
GRACE NOTES	$\mathcal{B}$y embracing life, we expand our consciousness. By taking everything seriously, we find "divinities in disguise" everywhere.	$\mathcal{R}$especting the opinions of others who think and have different views is stimulating. What's crucial is to *really* believe in what you espouse.	$\mathcal{W}$e form ourselves by our beliefs. In order to be authentic we have to find our own way, believing some things and disbelieving others.	$\mathcal{W}$hoever fed us the fantasy that life has a happy ending? Life is hard work and struggle. The more courageous you are, the happier you become.

	SUNDAY	MONDAY	TUESDAY	WEDNESDAY
MORNING	The first of earthly blessings, independence. EDWARD GIBBON			
NOON			Art is long and time is fleeting. LONGFELLOW	
AFTERNOON		We love being in love, that's the truth. THACKERAY		
EVENING				It is part of the cure to wish to be cured. SENECA
GRACE NOTES	Being self-sufficient is a powerful, freeing accomplishment. Love follows.	Being in love is a state of consciousness. We see and feel with a new awareness, a fresh appreciation. This week, *live* in love.	Creativity fluctuates. When you are in the flow of your art, give it your full force. "Time is fleeting."	Envision a pain-free, healthy body and heart. Never dwell on illness. Hide your prescriptions from view. Don't allow pity.

Thursday

Nothing is my last word about anything.   HENRY JAMES

Friday

In solitude alone can he know true freedom.
MONTAIGNE

Saturday

Men willingly believe what they wish.   JULIUS CAESAR

The purpose of life is not to be happy. The purpose of life is to matter, to be productive, to have it make some difference that you live at all.   LEO ROSTEN

THE BEST THINGS THAT HAPPENED THIS WEEK:

....
....
....
....
....
....
....

GOALS
FOR NEXT WEEK:

....
....
....
....
....
....
....

Insights are fluid. As we mature, we embrace a fresh point of view. We're free to change our minds.

Until we can embrace solitude without loneliness, we aren't free. Value inner resources as a great and noble virtue.

No intelligent, independent person embraces anything 100%. What we believe is private and can only be shared with our higher power.

Happiness is the result of pursuing your goals. Increase your usefulness. Happy?

THURSDAY

FRIDAY

The only gift is a portion of thyself. EMERSON

SATURDAY

For what is Mysticism? ...Is it not merely a hard word for "the kingdom of heaven is within"? Heaven is neither a place nor a time. FLORENCE NIGHTINGALE

THE BEST THINGS THAT HAPPENED THIS WEEK:

....
....
....
....
....
....
....

Don't look back. Something might be gaining on you. SATCHEL PAIGE

No one is free who commands not himself. EPICTETUS

GOALS
FOR NEXT WEEK:

....
....
....
....
....
....
....

Just do your best. This is all that we should ever expect from ourselves. Then let go. Believe in yourself and don't worry.

When we sincerely reach out, our gift is our vulnerability. Don't be afraid of rejection. Reach out.

Take your eyes off the other people in your life. Focus on yourself, only.

All the beauty, wonder and majesty you envision is where you are. God is not playing hide and seek. Heaven is already within.

INSIGHTS

It is not enough to stay busy. So, too, are the ants.
The question is what you are busy about.

—HENRY DAVID THOREAU

Half of the year is now over. Look back and analyze the content of your days—work, family, responsibilities, friends. What have been some of your best moments? Who were you with? Why?

The point is not simply to fill up your days. Benjamin Disraeli reminds us that "action may not always bring happiness, but there is no happiness without action." We must also raise the quality of each moment. When you rush about, scattered and exhausted, you are bound to be disappointed. Why wouldn't you be? We are often overambitious about how much we can take on, and therefore fall prey to unrealistic expectations.

Far better to simplify your schedule. Free yourself from self-imposed obligations and unwarranted responsibilities in order to take time to think about the meaning of your journey. Who are the people who enhance your life? What are the things that fulfill you rather than fill up time? What proportion of your time do you spend on your own activities, independent of a boss or a spouse or children? You may think that you should do more, when, in fact, you should be cutting back, readjusting your schedule to provide time for grace notes, insights and reflection. Age alone doesn't make us wise. We should engage in thoughtful meditation regularly.

Pay careful attention to the tugs in your soul. Value the time you spend peacefully without others as much as you look forward to true companionship and sharing. What we want is a balance that allows us to live in a state of soulful grace. It's not easy. It is up to you and you alone to clear the clutter from your path. You will never find time if you wait for a free moment. Take it. Seize it.

	*S*UNDAY	*M*ONDAY	*T*UESDAY	*W*EDNESDAY
MORNING	*W*ithout self-confidence we are as babes in the cradle. VIRGINIA WOOLF			*T*he first hour of the morning is the rudder of the day. BEECHER
NOON				
AFTERNOON		*W*hat mighty contests rise from trivial things. ALEXANDER POPE		
EVENING			*D*o what you can, with what you have, where you are. THEODORE ROOSEVELT	
GRACE NOTES	*C*onfidence is the result of awareness and achievement. Self-confidence builds.	*L*et small issues remain small. Before jumping into the fray, ask yourself how important it is.	*G*enius is making things work out. Don't make excuses for the failure to use wisely what you have. Make something of yourself.	*G*ive yourself the first hour every day. Make this a ritual. Look forward to meditating, reading, writing, walking in the quiet of early morning.

THURSDAY

$\mathcal{O}$ aching time! O moments big as years!
JOHN KEATS

FRIDAY

$\mathcal{D}$ ream lofty dreams and as you dream so shall you become.
JAMES ALLEN

SATURDAY

$\mathcal{I}$ have never found, in anything outside of the four walls of my study, an enjoyment equal to sitting at my writing-desk with a clean page, a new theme, and a mind awake.
WASHINGTON IRVING

$\mathcal{W}$ hen I work, I relax.
PICASSO

THE BEST THINGS THAT HAPPENED THIS WEEK:

....
....
....
....
....
....
....

GOALS
FOR NEXT WEEK:

❧...
....
....
....
❧...
....
....

$\mathcal{W}$ hen we are in pain, we feel time stretch eternally before us. Know that it shall pass.

$\mathcal{I}$ love to daydream. Before I go to sleep I program my dreams, thinking lofty thoughts. Keep a dream journal and you'll emulate them.

$\mathcal{W}$ hen I write, tension and stress fall away. What work do you do that soothes your nerves? Thinking without acting makes me nervous.

$\mathcal{W}$ hat solitary activity are you passionate about? Pursue your bliss and you'll be connected to a universal energy.

	SUNDAY	MONDAY	TUESDAY	WEDNESDAY
MORNING				*G*enius is the fire that lights itself. ANONYMOUS
NOON			*B*y a small sample we may judge of the whole piece. CERVANTES	
AFTERNOON		*T*he day may dawn when this plight shall be sweet to remember. VIRGIL		
EVENING	*I* am all ears. TROLLOPE			
GRACE NOTES	*W*hen we're alone we should listen to the stirrings of our soul. When we are among others we should be all ears, learning, growing, expanding.	*W*hen you feel you can't face life, toughen up. Be a fighter and life will be more meaningful because you have overcome the hurdle.	*Q*uality is consistent. You can judge someone's character without knowing everything. We often reveal all when we show a portion of ourselves.	*A*re you a self-starter? Do you wait for others to program you or do you take initiative? When an idea is yours, fire will appear.

THURSDAY

*W*e die only once, and for such a long time! MOLIÈRE

*W*e only live once, and for such a short time! Focus on our aliveness, our vital energy, and what we can accomplish here and now.

FRIDAY

*C*haracter is what you are in the dark. DWIGHT MOODY

*S*trive at all times to be yourself.

SATURDAY

*S*pontaneous courage. NAPOLEON

*W*e don't know when we'll be called upon to be brave. In acting strong we will tap into renewable energy. Fear not.

---

*H*appiness? It is an illusion to think that more comfort means more happiness. Happiness comes of the capacity to feel deeply, to enjoy simply, to think freely, to risk life, to be needed. STORM JAMESON

THE BEST THINGS THAT HAPPENED THIS WEEK:

....
....
....
....
....
....
....

GOALS
FOR NEXT WEEK:

❧..
....
....
....
❧..
....
....

*C*omfort is the reward of death, not life. Don't be fooled by so-called labor-saving devices. Use your body, your hands and your heart.

Month _____ THE WEEK OF _____ TO _____

	*S*UNDAY	*M*ONDAY	*T*UESDAY	*W*EDNESDAY
MORNING		*J*ust warm life… D. H. LAWRENCE		
NOON	*W*hat I cannot love, I overlook. ANAÏS NIN			*T*he *Two Ways:* One is to suffer; the other is to become a professor of the fact that another suffered. KIERKEGAARD
AFTERNOON				
EVENING			*T*he right time is anytime one is so lucky to be alive. HENRY JAMES	
GRACE NOTES	*T*hose whom we love we think about constantly. How many people do you love spiritually? We all hate to be overlooked.	*T*he greatest joy is that cozy feeling we get when we're able to relax at home.	*D*o you ever contemplate why you are lucky enough to be alive? No matter how challenging life is, we can always count our blessings.	*W*e are never alone in our suffering. Look into the eyes of anyone and feel their pain. Offer empathy and understanding.

THURSDAY

FRIDAY

L aughter is by definition healthy.   DORIS LESSING

SATURDAY

H e who hath a clear and lively imagination in his mind, may easily produce and utter the same.   MONTAIGNE

T oo busied with the crowded hour to fear to live or die.   EMERSON

THE BEST THINGS THAT HAPPENED THIS WEEK:

....

....

....

....

....

....

....

W e can never go back again, that much is certain.   DAPHNE DU MAURIER

GOALS
FOR NEXT WEEK:

➤..

....

....

....

➤..

....

....

W e have to make a conscious effort to live in the present. Understanding our history makes us move forward with vision and balance.

W hat makes you laugh? I hope many things. Laughter lightens our burdens and helps digestion.

T here's time for action and time for contemplation. Do not confuse the two.

B y thinking, reading, being curious and maintaining a childlike wonder, we fuel our imaginations. Write down some of your probing thoughts.

Month _____ THE WEEK OF _____ TO _____

	SUNDAY	MONDAY	TUESDAY	WEDNESDAY
MORNING			*Accept a miracle.* EDWARD YOUNG	
NOON				*One must keep ever present a sense of humor.* KATHERINE MANSFIELD
AFTERNOON		*Dreams are the touchstones of our characters.* THOREAU		
EVENING	*The way of the sage is to act but not to compete.* LAO-TZU			
GRACE NOTES	*We are not in competition. The way to success is to use our own talents, living up to our potential. This is a tall order.*	*Pay attention to your dreams. They are the keys to your subconscious. Use this real knowledge.*	*We shouldn't have to be hit over the head to believe in miracles. The birth of a child is enough proof; the telephone another.*	*It's difficult to spend much time with a person who is sullen. Humor delights us; we are drawn to it.*

THURSDAY

A distraction is to avoid the consciousness of the passage of time.

GERTRUDE STEIN

FRIDAY

*W*hen you come to the end of a perfect day...

CARRIE JACOBS BOND

SATURDAY

*G*ood fences make good neighbors.   ROBERT FROST

*T*he growth of wisdom may be gauged accurately by the decline of ill-temper.

NIETZSCHE

THE BEST THINGS THAT
HAPPENED THIS WEEK:

....
....
....
....
....
....
....

GOALS
FOR NEXT WEEK:

❧.......................................
....
....
....
❧.......................................
....
....

---

*D*istractions offer relief from the ordinary patterns of living. Then we want to get going again, refreshed.

*D*escribe what you consider a perfect day. Where are you? Who are you with? What are you up to? Can you make it happen?

*E*veryone feels more comfortable knowing their boundaries. Value others' privacy as you fiercely guard your own.

*D*o you know someone who is incessantly angry? Ill temper is a form of madness. Wisdom requires stability and a healthy attitude. Think wisely.

	SUNDAY	MONDAY	TUESDAY	WEDNESDAY
MORNING				*S*ing away sorrow, cast away care. CERVANTES
NOON	*W*ise men talk because they have something to say. PLATO		*T*o laugh is proper to man. RABELAIS	
AFTERNOON				
EVENING		*E*very sin is more injury to him who does than to him who suffers it. ST. AUGUSTINE		
GRACE NOTES	*I*t's not how much you say or how often, but what you think that matters. Wise people's conversation enhances our journey.	*T*o sin is to be off the path. Whenever someone is involved in any wrongdoing, they suffer. Pity those who are off their paths.	*L*aughter is always pleasurable. Laugh to cure your blues.	*S*ing in exaltation. While you sing, you celebrate. Let's sing together.

THURSDAY

Friendship needs a certain parallelism of life, a community of thought.
HENRY ADAMS

FRIDAY

Love is love's reward.
JOHN DRYDEN

SATURDAY

People often grudge others what they cannot enjoy themselves.
AESOP

Creativity comes when we allow our minds to wander freely.
MICHELE MCCORMICK

THE BEST THINGS THAT HAPPENED THIS WEEK:

....
....
....
....
....
....
....

GOALS
FOR NEXT WEEK:

❧...
....
....
....
❧...
....
....

We are friends with people because we share experiences, values and life-style. Call a good friend today.

Love is the ultimate feeling. When you love, you give of yourself. Be the loving one and experience rewards.

Share in a friend's joy and success. What they like is about them, not about you.

Everything is raw material to be molded and brought forth into a unique artistic expression. Look at everything with an open mind. Seek and be daring.

	SUNDAY	MONDAY	TUESDAY	WEDNESDAY
MORNING	*A*mbition is destruction; only competence matters. JILL ROBINSON			
NOON		*I* have freed my soul. ST. BERNARD		
AFTERNOON				*T*he work and the man are one. CARLOTTA MONTEREY O'NEILL
EVENING			*O*ne can acquire everything in solitude—except character. STENDAHL	
GRACE NOTES	*W*ork with discipline. Being good at what we choose to do with our talents is what matters. Burnished skill makes you competent.	*T*o feel an inner peace requires contemplation. Outer and inner conflicts abound. Have you made peace with all?	*C*haracter is formed step by small step in company and in solitude. Today use solitude to dream.	*N*ext to the word love, work is my favorite. We all do jobs in order to eat. Work is what we do to express ourselves.

THURSDAY

Discipline—in every way.
BROOKE ASTOR

FRIDAY

Effort, after days of laziness, seemed impossible.
DORIS LESSING

SATURDAY

Make haste slowly.
SUETONIUS

Someday I hope to enjoy enough of what the world calls success so that someone will ask me: "What's the secret of it?" I shall say simply this: "I get up when I fall down."
PAUL HARVEY

THE BEST THINGS THAT HAPPENED THIS WEEK:

....
....
....
....
....
....
....

GOALS
FOR NEXT WEEK:

....
....
....
....
....
....
....

Longevity, leadership and respect are not accidental. Discipline is the linchpin to a successful life. It is the rudder that keeps us on course.

One of the reasons artists and writers rarely take a day off is because they need to stay at the center of their efforts. Begin.

Move in the direction of your goal. Pace yourself for the finish. Timing, rhythm and ease are key.

When we were young, our mothers kissed our scratched knees. We were healed. Now we must heal ourselves.

Month _____ THE WEEK OF _____ TO _____

	SUNDAY	MONDAY	TUESDAY	WEDNESDAY
MORNING			*T*ry thinking of love, or something. CRISTOPHER FRY	
NOON	*A*lways to be best, and distinguished above the rest. HOMER			
AFTERNOON				*T*here is no wisdom in useless and hopeless sorrow. SAMUEL JOHNSON
EVENING		*L*ive in this moment and live in eternity. GOETHE		
GRACE NOTES	*E*veryone and everything plays a part in the human drama. Make a real contribution by being excellent. Shine.	*L*earn to live in an eternal now-ness. Concentrate on everything you see and do. Now. Now.	*W*e program our minds and hearts. Love is positive. Hate is negative. By thinking of love we become loving. Grace and joy result from loving.	*G*rieving, while unavoidable, must be transformed into strength and wisdom. Excess sorrow is the other side of joy. Choose joy.

THURSDAY

I do not understand;
I pause; I examine.   MONTAIGNE

FRIDAY

W hat tranquil joy his
friendly presence gives!
OLIVER WENDELL HOLMES

SATURDAY

S ickness need not be a part
of life.   ADELLE DAVIS

T he joy of life is
variety; the tenderest love
requires to be renewed by
intervals of absence.
SAMUEL JOHNSON

THE BEST THINGS THAT
HAPPENED THIS WEEK:

....
....
....
....
....
....
....

GOALS
FOR NEXT WEEK:

....
....
....
....
....
....

E veryone seems in a rush for
the answer. Who takes time to
examine the questions? We're
not born wise.

W hich of your friends
bring you joy by their mere
presence? Just thinking of
them will bring you peace,
contentment and hope.

T hink of living a long,
healthy life. Focus on energy,
vitality and optimism. Spread
joy and light. Take care of
your own health. Stay well.

W hen I am away from
loved ones, I appreciate their
qualities. When I'm with loved
ones, I enjoy them. Come,
share with me.

Month _____ THE WEEK OF _____ TO _____

	SUNDAY	MONDAY	TUESDAY	WEDNESDAY
MORNING				*T*hat is the road we all have to take. KIERKEGAARD
NOON				
AFTERNOON		*T*ime is the most valuable thing a man can spend. THEOPHRASTUS		
EVENING	*B*ring equal ease unto my pain. THOMAS CAREW		*L*et all things be done decently and in order. CORINTHIANS	
GRACE NOTES	*L*ife never gives us all pain or all pleasure. We all experience our share of challenges and disappointments as well as celebrations.	*A*t our deaths, we could have a fortune saved up. Time? We can't save it. Spend it well. Live it. Now.	*T*here is a divine order to all things. There is a right timing. What's next?	*O*ur daughter Brooke's metaphor for life is journey. Eliminate negative, poisonous energy along your road. Live.

Thursday

The life is short, the craft so long to learn. HIPPOCRATES

The sooner we find out what we're passionate about, the sooner we can learn our craft. We then get better at the art of living.

Friday

One thought fills immensity.
WILLIAM BLAKE

One clear thought may obliterate twenty years of muddle. What are you thinking?

Saturday

But above all, try something.
FRANKLIN DELANO ROOSEVELT

Ask yourself, What is the worst thing that could happen to you? Life well lived requires risks. Being afraid to try is a lost opportunity.

What kind of world would this be if everybody in it were just like me?
KANT

THE BEST THINGS THAT HAPPENED THIS WEEK:

....
....
....
....
....
....
....

GOALS
FOR NEXT WEEK:

❧..
....
....
....
❧..
....
....

Seek to find your uniqueness. Express your fire through color, cooking, writing or painting. Who *are* you?

	*S*UNDAY	*M*ONDAY	*T*UESDAY	*W*EDNESDAY
MORNING	*T*he reason of the strongest is always the best. JEAN DE LA FONTAINE			
NOON			*B*ut I have promises to keep/And miles to go before I sleep. ROBERT FROST	
AFTERNOON				*T*is always morning somewhere in the world. RICHARD HENRY HORNE
EVENING		*L*ife is the childhood of our immortality. GOETHE		
GRACE NOTES	*H*one your reasoning strengths. Until we can think clearly for ourselves, we will always depend on others.	*W*hatever good you do now will never die. We die; our virtue doesn't.	*W*e all have to get going. We've made promises to ourselves as well as to others. There is much we can accomplish before we sleep.	*S*ometimes we don't understand what is happening to us. What we see is not the whole picture. When it's dark, think of the sunshine.

THURSDAY

I believe because it is impossible.　TERTULLIAN

*W*e will never be able to figure everything out. But with faith, we can believe in the possible. Think of what you *can* do.

FRIDAY

*T*he time to relax is when you don't have time for it.
SYDNEY J. HARRIS

*T*he more we enjoy our daily activities, the more relaxation we will get from whatever we do. Take time to relax.

SATURDAY

*E*very day, in every way, I'm growing better and better.
ÉMILE COUÉ

*D*o you feel you are continuing to grow and stretch *every* day? When we are learning and acquiring wisdom, we *do* get better.

A vigorous five-mile walk will do more good for an unhappy but otherwise healthy adult than all the medicine and psychology in the world.
PAUL DUDLEY WHITE

THE BEST THINGS THAT
HAPPENED THIS WEEK:

....
....
....
....
....
....
....

GOALS
FOR NEXT WEEK:

....
....
....
....
....
....
....

*E*verything about walking is good for us. We clear our heads, invigorate our bodies and take time out. Let's go for a vigorous walk. Today.

	SUNDAY	_MONDAY_	_TUESDAY_	_WEDNESDAY_
MORNING			_V_irtue proceeds through effort. EURIPIDES	
NOON				
AFTERNOON		_I_t is not good to refuse a gift. HOMER		_E_ither a beast or a god. ARISTOTLE
EVENING	_T_hings do not change; we change. THOREAU			
GRACE NOTES	_W_e become more aware. We see things differently. Growth allows us to reconsider prior opinions. We grow wise as we change. Keep changing.	_N_ever be embarrassed by a genuine present. Receive it with grace.	_W_e don't become virtuous automatically. Whenever we make an effort, going the extra mile, we practice active virtue.	_T_he choice is usually not between two extremes. Practice generosity and kindness and you'll be closer to godliness.

THURSDAY

*L*et there be truth between us two forevermore.   EMERSON

*B*e a truth-seeker and a truth-bearer. You cannot control other people but you can face reality. Without truth there is no beauty.

FRIDAY

*L*ove, and do what you will.   ST. AUGUSTINE

*W*hatever you do, be in a loving frame of consciousness. Everything will then become sacred. Love is all we need.

SATURDAY

*L*eisure with dignity.   CICERO

*T*ake little private holidays. Treat yourself to some relaxed time when you free yourself of obligations. Create space for dignity and grace.

*N*o man who continues to add something to the material, intellectual and moral well-being of the place in which he lives is left long without proper reward.   BOOKER T. WASHINGTON

THE BEST THINGS THAT HAPPENED THIS WEEK:

....
....
....
....
....
....
....

GOALS FOR NEXT WEEK:

....
....
....
....
....
....
....

*R*ecognition is apt to follow excellence. Focus on all the modest, simple things you can do to add beauty, grace and joy. Reward yourself.

	SUNDAY	MONDAY	TUESDAY	WEDNESDAY
MORNING	He is well paid that is well satisfied. SHAKESPEARE		Let there be light. GENESIS	
NOON		Be a friend to yourself, and others will. SCOTTISH PROVERB		
AFTERNOON				
EVENING				Every house has a voice. LIZ SEYMOUR
GRACE NOTES	Whenever we feel fulfilled, we appreciate our lives. Like what you do; money will follow.	Every loving act you do for yourself is always translated into loving, generous acts of friendship.	Light a candle, symbol of an eternal flame. The flickering glow warms the heart and expands hope.	Every house speaks to us. Some sound sad while others sing out with joy. The difference between a house and a home is a voice.

THURSDAY

FRIDAY

To know that you do not know is the best. LAO-TZU

SATURDAY

I wish you some new love at lovely things/and some new forgetfulness at the teasing things/and some higher pride in the praising things/and some sweeter peace from the hurrying things/and some closer fence from the worrying things. JOHN RUSKIN

THE BEST THINGS THAT HAPPENED THIS WEEK:

....
....
....
....
....
....
....

Example is always more efficacious than precept.
SAMUEL JOHNSON

Love is a great beautifier.
LOUISA MAY ALCOTT

GOALS
FOR NEXT WEEK:

....
....
....
....
....
....
....

We are responsible for our acts and teach by example. Who are your mentors?

Even geniuses have blind spots. Do research. Ask for help. We'll never be bored trying to know more. Help!

Whether we love a child, another, or our work, there is a radiance about us that is beautiful. Think about all you love.

I wish you every goodness. I want your dreams to come true. May you soar with your own greatness, expand your essence and feel joy.

	SUNDAY	MONDAY	TUESDAY	WEDNESDAY
MORNING		*A* man of learning has riches within him. PHAEDRUS		
NOON			*I* f you rest, you rust. HELEN HAYES	
AFTERNOON				*W* isdom must be sought. EDWARD YOUNG
EVENING	*P* erform with all your heart your long and heavy task. ALFRED DE VIGNY			
GRACE NOTES	*C* oncentrated effort and determination never hurts us. Quitting too soon, losing focus, giving up break our hearts and ultimately kill us.	*O* ur inner treasures can go wherever we go without fear of theft. Make yourself beautiful with learning.	*K* eep climbing those mountains. We get energy from energy. Keep all your energy circuits lit up. Rest after death.	*Q* uestion everything. Do your own research. Use a variety of sources. Form your own opinions. Believe in your ability to become wise.

THURSDAY

*F*ailure is impossible.
SUSAN B. ANTHONY

*B*roaden your perspective. Have goals that enlarge you and make a difference. Study the lives of your heroes and heroines.

FRIDAY

*H*e is most powerful who has power over himself.
SENECA

*S*elf-control, self-resolve, self-confidence, self-respect, self-love equal self-power!

SATURDAY

*B*etter to light one candle than to curse the darkness.
THE CHRISTOPHERS

*T*he world is full of hopeless, faithless people. Think what you can do to spread light. Find solutions. Inspire a love of life.

*T*he only limit to our realization of tomorrow will be our doubts of today.

FRANKLIN DELANO ROOSEVELT

THE BEST THINGS THAT HAPPENED THIS WEEK:

....
....
....
....
....
....
....

GOALS FOR NEXT WEEK:

....
....
....
....
....
....
....

*I*t's natural, at times, to be afraid. The more we care, the more vulnerable we are. Never doubt your ability to make your *own* mark.

QUESTS

Life is a quest.

EDNA ST. VINCENT MILLAY

How do you feel about the first three-quarters of your year? This is the final stretch. No day can be repeated. Every act has consequences. Have you done something you're proud of? Have you taken on a project that means a great deal to you? What have been some of your goals? Have you been able to share in some good news of family and friends? How is your health? How is your energy?

No matter how much we identify with a spouse or child or our career, we should remember our own quests. What fills you with hope and what do you want to do in the short time left this year? This is your only lifetime. How intensely are you pursuing your goals?

Have you tried hard enough? When you need help, are you humble? Can you ask for assistance? When you feel discouraged, do you take time to reflect and let the pain teach you new dimensions of courage? Do you renew your faith in life regularly by counting your blessings and appreciating your hard-earned wisdom?

How much do you care about the quality of your daily journey? Do you have a ready smile, a bounce to your step, an enthusiasm about life that is infectious? Are you in control of your time? Do you arrange your schedule so you can thoughtfully pursue your interests, your passions, and increase your self-awareness?

Think of our lives as interconnecting circles. Every link is vital in the chain that binds us together. It is for us to make something of our being placed on earth at the same time. Find the reason. Let your journey through this world bring hope and faith, love and grace to you and those around you.

	SUNDAY	MONDAY	TUESDAY	WEDNESDAY
MORNING				
NOON				Nothing human is foreign to me. TERENCE
AFTERNOON	I am nearer home today than I have ever been before. PHOEBE CARY		It is certain because it is impossible. TERTULLIAN	
EVENING		I must find a way to live more simply. RUTH ST. DENIS		
GRACE NOTES	The essence of who we are becomes clear to us. We become whole and feel at home in our souls. How near home are you?	People clutter up their lives because they haven't found their inner fire. Once we discover our passion, we tend to simplify.	I like people with strong convictions and the fighting instinct to bring something forth. Without this faith, we collapse.	Living requires getting more than our hands dirty. Experience everything yourself. Trust your instincts.

THURSDAY	FRIDAY	SATURDAY	
	To look up is joy. CONFUCIUS		*I* love the man that can smile in trouble, that can gather strength from distress, and grow brave by reflection. THOMAS PAINE

THE BEST THINGS THAT
HAPPENED THIS WEEK:

....
....
....
....
....
....
....

Any excuse will serve a
tyrant.   AESOP

For man is man and master
of his fate.   TENNYSON

GOALS
FOR NEXT WEEK:

❧..
....
....
....
❧..
....
....

You can become as great
as you dare try. Death cannot
end your power to spread love.

Take a deep breath and
embrace the world around you.

You are in charge. Learn
from your mistakes. Grow.
Don't blame others. No
excuses.

Being gloomy never helps
a situation. A dying person
wants to be cheered up.
Grieve, reflect, then be strong
and brave. It's okay to smile.

Month _____   THE WEEK OF _____ TO _____

	SUNDAY	MONDAY	TUESDAY	WEDNESDAY
MORNING	*T*o be that self which one truly is. — KIERKEGAARD			*V*irtue is its own reward. — CICERO
NOON			*H*ear the other side. — ST. AUGUSTINE	
AFTERNOON				
EVENING		*N*othing short of independence, it appears to me, can possibly do. — GEORGE WASHINGTON		
GRACE NOTES	*P*retension is such a waste of everyone's time. The greater the person, the more genuine and authentic. Being true requires strict limits. Be *you*.	*B*eing free to act according to your beliefs is essential. Dictators come in all sizes and disguises. Don't accept any compromises. Fight.	*L*isten to the pain, the fear, the blindness, the anger as well as the reasoning behind someone's view. Hearing them out can clarify some differences.	*D*oing what's right, no matter how costly or painful, pays off; never compromise yourself out of fear or embarrassment.

THURSDAY	FRIDAY	SATURDAY	
			*O*pportunities are usually disguised as hard work, so most people don't recognize them. ANN LANDERS
	*I*f you are hungry, you're losing weight. PETER MEGARGEE BROWN		**THE BEST THINGS THAT HAPPENED THIS WEEK:** ....
*S*upreme impartiality is antihuman. GEORGE SAND			
	*W*e all die with our secret. BERTHE MORISOT		**GOALS FOR NEXT WEEK:** ....
*T*ake a stand. Cast your vote. Have a point of view. You don't have to be prejudiced to have an opinion. Allow subjectivity. It's honest.	*N*o need to tell all. We're allowed our private thoughts, our personal failures, regrets and longings. It doesn't bring back a loss to tell. Secret!	*D*on't eat unless you're hungry. Your stomach talks. No force-feedings.	*W*e've been tricked as a society to want ease. But opportunities that are easy aren't worth the trouble. Work!

Month _____ THE WEEK OF _____ TO _____

	SUNDAY	MONDAY	TUESDAY	WEDNESDAY
MORNING	*N*ot angles, but angels. GREGORY I		*W*hen soul is present, nature is alive. THOMAS MOORE	
NOON		*I*t is only to the individual that a soul is given. ALBERT EINSTEIN		
AFTERNOON				
EVENING				*P*raising what is lost makes the remembrance dear. SHAKESPEARE
GRACE NOTES	*C*oncentrate on angels. Think with a pure heart. Not everyone is looking for an angle. Become an earth angel. The world craves angels.	*B*elieving that there is a reason individuals possess a soul expands our spiritual horizons	*S*oul is the quintessence, the vital life force. Nature is soulful, alive, real, unending. Understand imperishable truth through nature.	*C*elebrating the life of a loved one keeps their spirit alive. Revitalize the life, not the death.

THURSDAY	FRIDAY	SATURDAY	
			If you would win a man to your cause, first convince him that you are his sincere friend. ABRAHAM LINCOLN
	Hurry is the weakness of fools. BALTASAR GRACIÁN		**THE BEST THINGS THAT HAPPENED THIS WEEK:** ....
I find nothing so dear as that which is given me. MONTAIGNE		*Talent* is best nurtured in solitude. GOETHE	
			GOALS FOR NEXT WEEK: ❧.................................... .... ❧.................................... ....
The art of appreciation is a sacred gift. Open up your arms and sing the praises of your many gifts. Hallelujah. Amen.	*Where* are we headed? What's the hurry? We become scattered when we rush about. It makes us anxious. Gentle swiftness.	*When* we're constantly hanging around people, we're not able to develop our talent. We nurture potential in solitude.	*Until* we know you really care about us we will not easily be convinced about anything. Most of us are open to a sincere friend's cause.

Month _____ THE WEEK OF _____ TO _____

	SUNDAY	MONDAY	TUESDAY	WEDNESDAY
MORNING				*W*e know the truth, not only by reason, but by the heart. PASCAL
NOON				
AFTERNOON		*W*e are always the same age inside. GERTRUDE STEIN		
EVENING	*W*hat wisdom can you find that is greater than kindness? JEAN-JACQUES ROUSSEAU		*U*ncertainty and expectation are the joys of life. WILLIAM CONGREVE	
GRACE NOTES	*A*ny kindness you experience or extend is grace. Touch a heart with your kindest self.	*N*ow that my daughters are adults, our age difference seems to melt away. We share jewelry, scarves and confidences. Inner agelessness transcends age.	*M*ay your future days be filled with uncertainty so you have the thrill of anticipation and expectation. Let joy fill your days.	*W*hen our heart aches we don't always understand why. But truth tugs at us and forces us to pay attention. Truth is deeply felt.

THURSDAY	FRIDAY	SATURDAY	
		*N*othing can be created out of nothing. LUCRETIUS	*O*nly in growth, reform and change, paradoxically enough, is true security to be found. ANNE MORROW LINDBERGH
*A*s for me, prizes mean nothing. My prize is my work. KATHARINE HEPBURN			**THE BEST THINGS THAT HAPPENED THIS WEEK:** ....
	*E*xuberance is beauty. WILLIAM BLAKE		
			GOALS FOR NEXT WEEK: ....
*N*o prize is meaningful unless it is deserved. The work that created the award is the life force. What is your prize? Your work?	*W*hatever you are enthusiastic about will make you beautiful. The more exuberant, the more beautiful.	*B*e active about your desires. Make things happen for you. Send your ship out to sail. And don't be afraid of rejection.	*W*hy are we afraid of change? Circumstances are always changing. We must take risks, embrace change.

	SUNDAY	MONDAY	TUESDAY	WEDNESDAY
MORNING		*I* like to be distinguished. MOLIÈRE		*S*peech is the picture of the mind. JOHN KAY
NOON	*I*n the beginning was the word. JOHN			
AFTERNOON				
EVENING			*O*n this whirligig of time we circle with the seasons. TENNYSON	
GRACE NOTES	*S*ince you've grown up, how many of your childhood beliefs have you shed? How much time do you set aside for meditation?	*B*eing accomplished and acclaimed in a specialty feels good. Don't be shy in accepting praise.	*E*verything is a circle. We need to find the connecting links. As the seasons come and go, they teach us faith, hope, love and change.	*W*e communicate our thoughts when we talk and write. Pay attention to your mind. Think beautiful thoughts.

THURSDAY	FRIDAY	SATURDAY	
			*E*ach morning see a task begun, each evening see it close. Something attempted, something done, has earned a night's repose. LONGFELLOW
		*W*hat I long for I have. NARCISSUS	THE BEST THINGS THAT HAPPENED THIS WEEK: ....
*H*onor is simply the morality of superior men. H. L. MENCKEN			
	I am independent! I can live alone and I love to work. MARY CASSATT		GOALS FOR NEXT WEEK: ❧... .... ❧... ....
*W*e dignify ourselves when we show proper respect for others. Looking up to certain people elevates our sights.	*F*ew people can claim such freedom. Each of us should be prepared to live alone.	*W*hat are your unmet needs and longings? I feel complete now that we've found our seaside cottage. Do you have what you long for?	*T*here is satisfaction in completion. We need closure to feel accomplishment. Begin one thing each day and finish it before you sleep.

Month _____ THE WEEK OF _____ TO _____

	*S*UNDAY	*M*ONDAY	*T*UESDAY	*W*EDNESDAY
MORNING			*N*o man is wise enough by himself. TITUS MACCIUS PLAUTUS	
NOON		*I*t's futile to have regrets. HELENE HANFF		
AFTERNOON				*J*oy is a net of love by which you can catch souls. MOTHER TERESA
EVENING	*T*he two noblest of things…are sweetness and light. JONATHAN SWIFT			
GRACE NOTES	*L*ook for sweet things as well as people. Sweetness is never mean or sour. Light puts a smile on everything. Sweetness and light to you.	*R*egrets are so passive. You can't do anything. Focus on now, what actions you can take. Live with as few regrets as possible.	*T*hink of all your teachers, those grace-bearers in your life who have guided you, encouraged you, loved you and inspired you. Give thanks.	*M*other Teresa persuaded a tearful volunteer to stay by saying, "We're not afraid here; we love and heal."

THURSDAY	FRIDAY	SATURDAY	
	It's later than you think. WRITING ON A CHINESE WALL		*People are ridiculous only when they try to seem or to be that which they are not.* GIACOMO LEOPARDI

We are always getting ready to live, but never living.
EMERSON

THE BEST THINGS THAT HAPPENED THIS WEEK:

....
....
....
....
....
....
....

In the long run, men only hit what they aim at.
THOREAU

GOALS FOR NEXT WEEK:

❧..
....
....
....
❧..
....
....

Jump right in and live now. There will never be a better time. You will never be the same person. Catch life on the fly.

Every day be conscious of the shortness of life and the limits of time. Take nothing for granted. Each day is a precious gift.

Set your sights high. If you do achieve all your goals you will surprise yourself by the joy in your accomplishments. Hit the mark!

Why are people so dissatisfied with themselves? Seek authenticity, honesty and truth. Be that real person you are.

Month _____ THE WEEK OF _____ TO _____

	*S*UNDAY	*M*ONDAY	*T*UESDAY	*W*EDNESDAY
MORNING	*L*ife is either a daring adventure or it is nothing. HELEN KELLER			
NOON		*O*ur sight is the most perfect and most delightful of all our senses. JOSEPH ADDISON		*J*oy is a flame in me too steady to destroy. SARA TEASDALE
AFTERNOON			*K*nowledge and human power are synonymous. FRANCIS BACON	
EVENING				
GRACE NOTES	*I*t requires daring to be yourself. Life isn't for sissies. Live deeply, dare beautifully and enjoy life's adventure.	*H*elen Keller never had sight, yet she brought great insights and guts to bear on her life. Use your eyes to *really* see.	*B*e a student of life. Freedom is earned, not granted. Learn, digest and have power.	*K*eep the flame of joy in your heart. Don't let setbacks, disappointments or world events rob you of your moments of joy. Joy is grace.

$\mathcal{T}$HURSDAY	$\mathcal{F}$RIDAY	$\mathcal{S}$ATURDAY	

$\mathcal{I}$ am always with myself, and it is I who am my tormentor. TOLSTOI

$\mathcal{R}$isk! Risk anything! Care no more for the opinions of others, for those voices. Do the hardest thing on earth for you. Act for yourself. Face the truth.

KATHERINE MANSFIELD

THE BEST THINGS THAT HAPPENED THIS WEEK:

....
....
....
....
....
....
....

$\mathcal{F}$aith which does not doubt is dead faith.

MIGUEL DE UNAMUNO

$\mathcal{A}$ll the pleasure of life is in general ideas.

OLIVER WENDELL HOLMES

GOALS
FOR NEXT WEEK:

....
....
....
....
....
....
....

$\mathcal{B}$eing interested in all kinds of ideas provides a great deal of pleasure wherever you are. Open yourself up to new interests every day.

$\mathcal{D}$oubt makes us think. Doubt helps confim our beliefs.

$\mathcal{H}$ow often do you consider who your true companion is? Day, night, weeks, months, years, decades—a lifetime of you. Become your best friend.

$\mathcal{L}$ife lived fully is a risky adventure. Stretch yourself. Don't wait for approval. Pay no attention to doubting Thomas. Act, risk, dare—live.

Month _____ THE WEEK OF _____ TO _____

	SUNDAY	MONDAY	TUESDAY	WEDNESDAY
MORNING	The ancestor of every action is a thought. EMERSON			What I give, I give freely. ELEANOR ROOSEVELT
NOON			Ye immortal gods, where in the world are we? CICERO	
AFTERNOON				
EVENING		. . .The never-ending flight of future days. JOHN MILTON		
GRACE NOTES	Aristotle believed in active virtue. Don't hesitate to follow up on your thoughts. What you think becomes who you are.	All our days will fly by whether we have anything exciting to record or not. By keeping a journal or a book of days, we magnify time.	Today the world spins so rapidly. We wonder where we are and where we're going. Pay attention to universal truths and to preserving civilization.	Never follow a gift. Enjoy the pleasure of giving and let go. Don't cling. Make anonymous donations to charities.

THURSDAY	FRIDAY	SATURDAY	

*M*y own conviction has always been to seek the inner reality, with the belief that the fruits of future values will be able to grow only after they are sown by the values of our history.

ROLLO MAY

*T*hese things were permanent, they could not be dissolved.   DAPHNE DU MAURIER

THE BEST THINGS THAT HAPPENED THIS WEEK:

....
....
....
....
....
....
....

I think, therefore I am.

DESCARTES

A man dishonored is worse than dead.   CERVANTES

GOALS
FOR NEXT WEEK:

....
....
....
....
....
....
....

*D*on't do anything to dishonor yourself. Character, virtue, integrity, honesty and truth are more sacred than anything else.

*W*e are the essence of our thoughts. Believing in the goodness of our fellow human beings keeps discouragement at bay.

*T*here are a lot of things of value that cannot be replaced. What are the principles most permanent in your life? Faith, hope, truth, love?

*W*e live in our own time. We can only respond responsibly to the reality we experience. Future values, if different, will take care of themselves.

	SUNDAY	MONDAY	TUESDAY	WEDNESDAY
MORNING			Heaven from all creatures hides the book of fate. ALEXANDER POPE	
NOON		Every beginning is hard. GERMAN PROVERB		
AFTERNOON	In a man's letters his soul lies naked. SAMUEL JOHNSON			
EVENING				He who has begun his task has half done it. Have the courage to be wise. HORACE
GRACE NOTES	Whether we write a love letter, a journal, a newspaper column, an essay or a book, we expose our inner selves. Are you willing?	Every self-doubt and fear is magnified in the void prior to our beginning. Start today. Greatness builds from a leap of faith and commitment.	People defuse death's sting by thinking about heaven. Our fate is to die. Can heavenly angels change this reality?	Remember there are no pure beginnings. We're already in the throes of things. Just do it. Don't wait until it's impossible. Be wise. Begin.

Month _____ THE WEEK OF _____ TO _____

THURSDAY	FRIDAY	SATURDAY	
		*F*ind your inner light and shine it on others. ELISABETH CAREY LEWIS	*E*xample is not the main thing in life…it is the only thing. ALBERT SCHWEITZER
	*T*he essential thing is the life of the individual. JUNG		**THE BEST THINGS THAT HAPPENED THIS WEEK:** ....
*I*magination is more important than knowledge. ALBERT EINSTEIN			
			GOALS FOR NEXT WEEK: ....
*D*on't wait for knowledge to come to you. Imagine situations. Visualize events. Are you a storyteller? What's the scenario?	*W*hen you are concerned enough to take care of yourself, everything else seems to fall into place. This is up to each individual to do.	*T*he only true happiness comes from self-illumination that can be shared with others. The more we discover, the more we can give away.	*L*ittle is learned from hypocrites. We don't gain inspiration from a deceiver or a cheat. Genuinely loving actions light our path.

Month _____ THE WEEK OF _____ TO _____

	*S*UNDAY	*M*ONDAY	*T*UESDAY	*W*EDNESDAY
MORNING	*T*hey can because they think they can. VIRGIL			
NOON		*A*s men, we are all equal in the presence of death. PUBLILIUS SYRUS		*E*xistence is always in process of self-transcending. ROLLO MAY
AFTERNOON				
EVENING			*T*here are two kinds of beauty—loveliness and dignity. CICERO	
GRACE NOTES	*M*y favorite childhood book was *The Little Engine That Could.* Think you can, and you can. "I think I can… I thought I could." Try.	*L*ook into the eyes of a friend or neighbor and understand *their* journey. We are all together here on earth, now and in death.	*L*oveliness doesn't automatically give one dignity. What respect you have for yourself and are granted by others is high beauty.	*W*e never have to be stuck in a rut. Change can be disquieting, but it always opens doors to growth.

THURSDAY	FRIDAY	SATURDAY	
			*K*eep your fears to yourself but share your courage with others. ROBERT LOUIS STEVENSON

THE BEST THINGS THAT
HAPPENED THIS WEEK:

....
....
....
....
....
....
....

*N*o, I ask it for the knowledge of a lifetime.
WHISTLER

*T*he greater man the greater courtesy.   TENNYSON

*S*o even in despair, man and woman must laugh.
LIN YUTANG

GOALS
FOR NEXT WEEK:

➤...
....
....
....
➤...
....
....

*C*reative people cannot be properly paid by the hour. What seems to be the result of a burst of inspiration took a lifetime.

*W*e can't take life and our present situation *too* seriously. A little laughter helps ease the pain.

*P*eople who are really accomplished tend to be considerate and generous. Emulate them.

*A*ssume we are all frightened of something. When someone shares a courageous act with us, we are strengthened.

	*S*UNDAY	*M*ONDAY	*T*UESDAY	*W*EDNESDAY
MORNING		*H*e that increaseth knowledge increaseth sorrow. ECCLESIASTES		
NOON	*I*f you want to be happy, be. TOLSTOI		*M*ake yourself necessary to somebody. EMERSON	
AFTERNOON				
EVENING				*B*e sure you are right; then go ahead. DAVID CROCKETT
GRACE NOTES	*W*hat's keeping you from having a marvelous day? Don't let troubles weigh you down. Choose happiness.	*I*n gaining knowledge we learn about pain but also about joy. Choose knowledge.	*W*henever we connect, we assume a responsibility for others. Be accountable and responsive.	*W*henever you research something and believe it is right for you at the time, make a commitment in good faith.

THURSDAY	FRIDAY	SATURDAY	
	*V*ision is the art of seeing things invisible. JONATHAN SWIFT		*W*hat would you attempt to do if you knew you could not fail? ROBERT SCHULLER
		*L*ove is a force. ANNE MORROW LINDBERGH	THE BEST THINGS THAT HAPPENED THIS WEEK: ....
A teacher affects eternity. HENRY BROOKS ADAMS			
			GOALS FOR NEXT WEEK: ....
*A*ll of us have power to influence others positively or negatively. Teach truth kindly.	*T*rue vision requires faith and imagination. Reality is far too complex to comprehend completely. Give in to the mystery.	*D*on't always insist on being logical, rational and sensible. When you are in the force of love, you will know great power.	*F*ailure begins with letting fear rule you. Whenever we try, no matter what we attempt, if we stick with it we won't fail. What will you try?

	*S*UNDAY	*M*ONDAY	*T*UESDAY	*W*EDNESDAY
MORNING	*F*irst…go to the light. ANTHONY B. PETRO			*I* don't wish you anything but just what you are—. IBSEN
NOON				
AFTERNOON			*C*hange the name, and the tale is about you.　HORACE	
EVENING		*I*t all began so beautifully. LADY BIRD JOHNSON		
GRACE NOTES	*L*ight is glory. As soon as you wake up, get a cup of coffee and go to a window or outside to experience the light.	*N*o one knows what is going to happen. We take risks, do what we believe is right for us and take our chances. Begin beautifully.	*D*o you identify with others? Imagining ourselves in other people's situations helps us appreciate our own predicament.	*S*tay as caring and genuine as you are today, always. Your smile, your enthusiasm and warmth uplift the lives of everyone around you.

$\mathcal{T}$HURSDAY	$\mathcal{F}$RIDAY	$\mathcal{S}$ATURDAY	
			$\mathcal{N}$othing is so strong as gentleness; nothing so gentle as real strength. ST. FRANCIS DE SALES
$\mathcal{S}$elf-respect—that cornerstone of all virtue. JOHN HERSCHEL		$\mathcal{W}$hat is beautiful is moral, that is all there is to it. FLAUBERT	**THE BEST THINGS THAT HAPPENED THIS WEEK:** ....
	$\mathcal{T}$he good lives on and does us all some good. RUTH GORDON		
			GOALS FOR NEXT WEEK: ....
$\mathcal{W}$hen we become our own friend, we esteem ourselves. Self-respect is the armor of the soul.	$\mathcal{G}$ood men and women continue to guide our course hundreds of years later. What good do you want to pass on to future generations?	$\mathcal{T}$rue beauty is moral. Strive to make your world more beautiful.	$\mathcal{A}$ gentle person is not out to prove anything. That's true courage.

	SUNDAY	MONDAY	TUESDAY	WEDNESDAY
MORNING	*We* don't know who we are until we see what we can do. MARTHA GRIMES			
NOON			*I* am at war 'twixt will and will not. SHAKESPEARE	
AFTERNOON				*H*onesty is the first chapter of the book of wisdom. THOMAS JEFFERSON
EVENING		*T*he great end of life is not knowledge but action. THOMAS HUXLEY		
GRACE NOTES	*S*elf-discovery comes through our actions. What is keeping you from doing all the exciting things you dream of? See what *you* can do. Know.	*K*nowledge alone is passive. Until you use your unique talents and bring something forth, you're wasting your life.	*I*ndecision cripples. Are you constantly changing your mind? Do you buy things and then return them? Choose. Don't wobble.	*I*'m nervous around people I can't trust. I sense something is off even when I'm being treacherously charmed. Honesty is essential.

THURSDAY	FRIDAY	SATURDAY	
		… Grace upon grace … JOHN BOWEN COBURN	*I* slept and dreamt that life was joy. I woke and saw that life was duty. I acted, and behold! Duty was joy. RABINDRANATH TAGORE
	H old thou the good: define it well. TENNYSON		THE BEST THINGS THAT HAPPENED THIS WEEK: ....
E verything we do has a result. GOETHE			GOALS FOR NEXT WEEK: ❧...................................... .... ❧...................................... ....
T here are consequences for every action. Think ahead. That's the definition of responsibility.	*F* ocus on goodness. What is good? How does it affect you? How does the lack of good make you feel? You always know good. True?	*G* race is a gift from God, freely given us. Be open and ready to receive grace. Count hundreds of grace notes every day.	*A* ll duty is an opportunity to serve, to give thanks, to give back and to appreciate. Use yourself well in duty. Joy always follows.

BIRTHDAYS AND CELEBRATIONS

January

DATE   EVENT

_____

_____

_____

_____

_____

_____

_____

_____

_____

_____

_____

_____

February

DATE   EVENT

_____

_____

_____

_____

_____

_____

_____

_____

_____

_____

_____

_____

March

DATE   EVENT

_____

_____

_____

_____

_____

_____

_____

_____

_____

_____

_____

_____

July

DATE   EVENT

_____

_____

_____

_____

_____

_____

_____

_____

_____

_____

_____

_____

August

DATE   EVENT

_____

_____

_____

_____

_____

_____

_____

_____

_____

_____

_____

_____

September

DATE   EVENT

_____

_____

_____

_____

_____

_____

_____

_____

_____

_____

_____

_____

April

DATE	EVENT

May

DATE	EVENT

June

DATE	EVENT

October

DATE	EVENT

November

DATE	EVENT

December

DATE	EVENT

Children's, Lovers', and Friends' Favorites

CHILD
FAVORITE THINGS

LOVER
FAVORITE THINGS

FRIEND
FAVORITE THINGS

CHILD
FAVORITE THINGS

LOVER
FAVORITE THINGS

LOVER
FAVORITE THINGS

FRIEND
FAVORITE THINGS

CHILD
FAVORITE THINGS

LOVER
FAVORITE THINGS

FRIEND
FAVORITE THINGS

CHILD

FAVORITE THINGS

_____

LOVER

FAVORITE THINGS

_____

FRIEND

FAVORITE THINGS

_____

FRIEND

FAVORITE THINGS

_____

CHILD

FAVORITE THINGS

_____

LOVER

FAVORITE THINGS

_____

FRIEND

FAVORITE THINGS

_____

CHILD

FAVORITE THINGS

_____

CHILD

FAVORITE THINGS

_____

LOVER

FAVORITE THINGS

_____

 IVING  IFTS

GIFT	FOR	WHERE PURCHASED	WHEN GIVEN

GIFTS READY TO GIVE!

GIFT   WHERE STORED

QUOTES, AFFIRMATIONS AND INSPIRATIONS

$\mathcal{L}$AUGHTER (Stories that made you laugh)

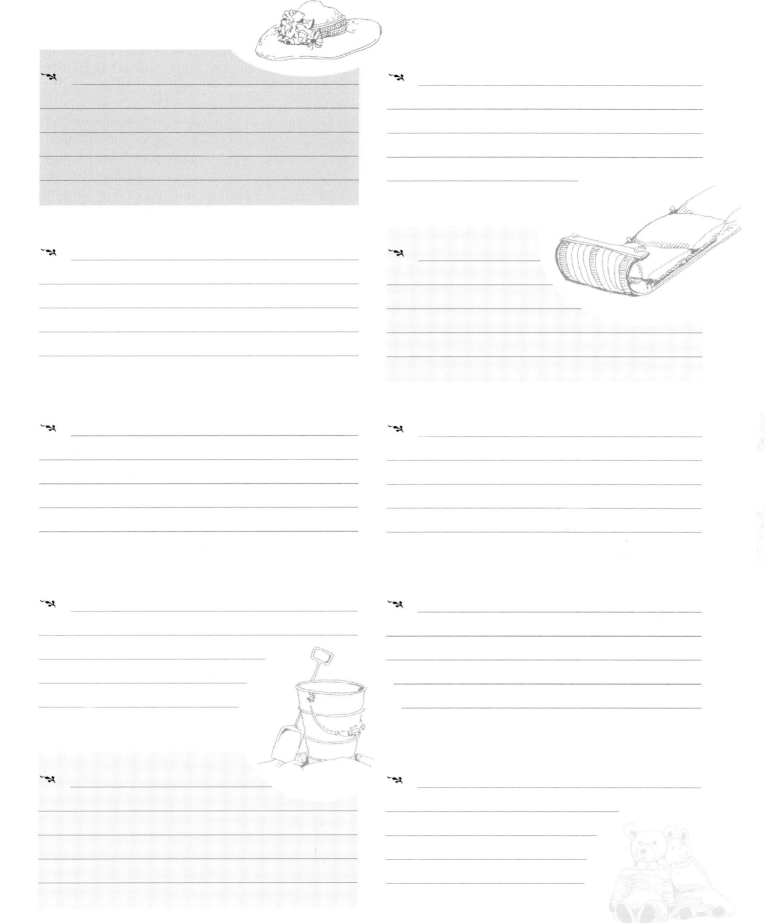

Joys, Sorrows and Things Learned

CARING, FOR YOURSELF ...

DOCTOR: _____

PHONE: _____

NOTES: _____

_____

DOCTOR: _____

PHONE: _____

NOTES: _____

_____

EYE DOCTOR: _____

PHONE: _____

NOTES: _____

_____

SPECIALIST: _____

PHONE: _____

NOTES: _____

_____

COUNSELOR: _____

PHONE: _____

NOTES: _____

_____

VETERINARIAN: _____

PHONE: _____

NOTES: _____

_____

DOCTOR: _____

PHONE: _____

NOTES: _____

_____

DENTIST: _____

PHONE: _____

NOTES: _____

_____

LAWYER: _____

PHONE: _____

NOTES: _____

_____

GYM/TRAINER: _____

PHONE: _____

NOTES: _____

_____

HAIRDRESSER: _____

PHONE: _____

NOTES: _____

_____

OTHER: _____

PHONE: _____

NOTES: _____

_____

AND Your Home

AUTO REPAIR: _____

PHONE: _____

NOTES: _____

_____

PLUMBER: _____

PHONE: _____

NOTES: _____

_____

ELECTRICIAN: _____

PHONE: _____

NOTES: _____

_____

HANDYMAN: _____

PHONE: _____

NOTES: _____

_____

PAINTER: _____

PHONE: _____

NOTES: _____

_____

YARD WORK: _____

PHONE: _____

NOTES: _____

_____

HOME INSURANCE: _____

PHONE: _____

NOTES: _____

_____

HARDWARE STORE: _____

PHONE: _____

NOTES: _____

_____

BANK: _____

PHONE: _____

NOTES: _____

_____

PHARMACY: _____

PHONE: _____

NOTES: _____

_____

SECURITY CO.: _____

PHONE: _____

NOTES: _____

_____

OTHER: _____

PHONE: _____

NOTES: _____

_____

ASPIRATIONS

$\mathscr{B}$OOKS I HAVE READ

$\mathscr{B}$OOKS I WANT TO READ

Notes

NOTES

NOTES